A Witches' Book of Ghosts and Exorcism

Previous books by Robin Skelton

SPELLCRAFT
TALISMANIC MAGIC
THE PRACTICE OF WITCHCRAFT TODAY

A Witches' Book of Ghosts and Exorcism

Robin Skelton
and
Jean Kozocari

ROBERT HALE · LONDON

First published in Great Britain 1990

ISBN 0 7090 4024 5

CIP Data to Follow

Robert Hale Limited
Clerkenwell House
Clerkenwell Green
London EC1R 0HT

Photoset in Ehrhardt by
Derek Doyle & Associates, Mold, Clwyd.
Printed in Great Britain by
St Edmundsbury Press Ltd, Bury St Edmunds, Suffolk.
Bound by WBC Bookbinders Limited.

Contents

Preface

Recently, and not entirely seriously, I described myself to someone as a Consultant Witch. The term is much more applicable, however, to Jean Kozocari, who, because of her abilities as a psychic and her knowledge of all things pertaining to the occult, is constantly being asked for her help and advice not only by private individuals but also by the police. Moreover, her frequent participation in radio programmes across Canada, and her television appearances, have established her as an authority to whom people naturally turn when they are troubled by what appear to them to be supernatural disturbances.

We both live in the city of Victoria on Vancouver Island in British Columbia, and almost all the hauntings we describe in this book have taken place here. Victoria is the provincial capital of British Columbia and is a relatively small city famous for its abundance of trees and its gardens. It began its separate identity as a place on 13 March 1843 when the Hudson Bay's chief factor, *James Douglas*, anchored off what became known as Shoal Point, Victoria Harbour. A Hudson Bay fort was soon established and the city began its career as, first, a fur-trading post, and later the main jumping-off point for the gold rush that occurred on the mainland in the late 1850s. For a time Victoria boasted the largest Chinatown on the west coast of North America, though its Chinatown now is relatively small. Vancouver Island, a separate colony, was unified with the mainland colony of British Columbia in 1866, and in 1867 Victoria became the provincial capital. On 20 July 1871, British Columbia joined the Dominion of Canada.

From this time onwards, Victoria was an established haven for many kinds of people. Its 'Englishness' was commented on by a number of people but Kipling wrote of it: 'To realize Victoria you must take all that the eye admires most in Bournmouth, Torquay, the Isle of Wight, the Happy Valley at Hong Kong – the Doon, Sorrento, and Camps Bay; add reminiscences of the Bay of Naples, with some Himalayas in the background.' The city attracted many people, including wealthy farmers from the Prairies eager to miss the harsh winters, and also families returning from India and Asia. The climate is temperate; it's a terrible winter if there is snow on the ground for more than ten days. Greater Victoria is now considered as including the municipalities of Esquimalt, where there is a naval base, and Oak Bay which contains many of the city's oldest and most impressive houses. To the north of Oak Bay, the municipality of Saanich contains the University of Victoria. The city is twenty minutes away from a countryside made dramatic by mountains, lakes, and forests. It is a place to fall in love with, as I did when I first visited it in 1962, and I was overjoyed to make my home there permanently the following year.

Vancouver Island now has more native Indian inhabitants than any other place in Canada, apart from the junctions of the Great Lakes, and the various Indian peoples – the Coast Salish, the Nootka, the Kwakiutl – have a rich tradition of myth and legend and an intense spiritual life. This is an important thread in the tapestry which is Victoria. Sailors provide another element in the web; Victoria has many stories of the sea, and the west coast of Vancouver Island is notorious for the number of shipwrecks that have happened there. Add to these, the rich mixture of cultures provided by a population which includes immigrants or descendants of immigrants from almost all corners of the world, and more artists, writers, craftspeople, antique shops and bookstores than any city of comparable size in the country, and you have a city where almost anything could happen, and frequently does. Moreover, Victoria has a strong pagan community, and while it cannot reasonably be regarded as the Witchcraft Capital of Canada, as it has been termed by some journalists, it is certainly a place where witches feel at home, as do Jean Kozocari and myself.

Jean can trace her family involvement with witchcraft back to the fifteenth century, and her familiarity with hauntings began in her childhood. My own involvement in the subject began much later in my life, though as a child and a young man I did have a number of experiences which, in hindsight, I now realize were encounters with the world of spirits. It was not until I met Jean Kozocari, and myself became initiated as a witch, that I discovered my own talents as a ghost-hunter, however. I had practised and researched other witchcraft skills for some years, and did, indeed, produce three books on the subject – *Spellcraft* (1978), *Talismanic Magic* (1985) and *The Practice of Witchcraft Today* (1988), but I had not tackled the subject of ghosts.

I do not need to describe my first experience of exorcism here, for I have told the story elsewhere in the book, in Chapter 3. Since that time I have worked on many hauntings, sometimes alone but mostly with Jean. This book is a selection of our adventures.

Because there is so much confusion about ghosts and their nature, we have attempted to give a clear account of the different types of haunting and to illustrate each type from our own experience. We have also given a detailed description of a full rite of exorcism. This rite, like many of the lesser rites presented here, is couched in terms of our religion, the old pre-Christian religion of witches. Anyone who finds our terminology strange, and therefore cannot easily make use of the ceremonies we suggest for use, may alter them without changing their effectiveness, providing the revised versions follow the same principles as the originals. As William Blake pointed out, 'All Religions are One', and it makes little difference whether one exorcizes a ghost in the name of one deity or another, as long as one believes in the power of that deity or that spiritual force.

A complete full-scale exorcism is only occasionally necessary in dealing with ghosts, as our experiences testify. Quite often a troublesome haunting can be dealt with very simply indeed.

Sometimes, however, not even a full-scale exorcism will be successful, and we have taken care to include in this book some examples of our failures as well as our successes. We have mentioned one or two hauntings with which we have not been personally involved, in order to illustrate the rich variety of types of haunting, but we have given only one or two, for we feel it is important to present first-hand accounts, and not accounts which have been filtered down through time and become distorted as a consequence. Many stories of ghosts have, we feel, been presented as if the whole thing is inexplicable or can, at best, be explained by saying that someone was murdered and therefore haunts the place of death, or that this place is haunted by the ghost of a suicide, as if that were in itself sufficient to indicate the reason for the appearance of a spectre. Ghosts do not appear without reason; there is always an explanation, and we have done our best to give explanations wherever possible, or at least present informed speculation. We have not, we believe, fallen for that enthusiasm of Sir Thomas Browne, who loved to pursue his reason 'to an O Altitudo', but have always sought commonsense explanations first of all.

In making this book we have followed a simple method. When the experience has been solely Jean's, I have tape-recorded her account and based my writing upon a transcript, which she has, of course, checked, and where her own words seemed to me to be most valuable, as in her description of emotions or psychic perceptions, I have quoted her direct. In those cases where we have both been involved, I have given both our points of view, for no two people ever have exactly the same experience in any situation, especially in one involving psychic awareness.

I have avoided that use of hyperbole which afflicts so many accounts of ghosts. I do not believe that I have used the word 'ghastly' at all, and I have used 'horror' and 'terror' only when wholly appropriate.

We have been helped by a number of people in recalling details of these experiences which we ourselves did not recall precisely, and we must thank Jean's daughter Tara and my wife Sylvia in particular for having, on several occasions, reminded us of crucial details. We are very grateful to Marilyn Bowering and Leon Reed for contributing their own personal experiences. We must also thank Charles Lillard for giving us the benefit of his vast knowledge of local history, and all those people who allowed us to use their actual names.

We have not been able to use actual names and addresses all the time, for some of those whom we have helped rid themselves of ghosts feel, quite understandably, that they do not wish to become publicly known as people who have had experiences of this kind; they would rather not risk the notoriety that this might bring. Others feel, again understandably, that our announcement that their home has been haunted might bring down real-estate values. Nevertheless there are living witnesses to all the events we describe, and we hope that the number of names we have been able to publish will satisfy all but dyed-in-the-wool sceptics.

We should perhaps be explicit here, however. The following names are fiction, though their reported experiences are not. In Chapter 1, John and Margaret; in Chapter 2, Beth, George, Elizabeth, Jill and Sandy, in Chapter 3, Donna and Bill; in Chapter 6, Mr Jones and Mr and Mrs Peters; in Chapter 8, Brenda and Mr and Mrs Barber, in Chapter 9, Arthur, Nancy, and Tom; and in Chapter 10, Mr and Mrs Green.

There is nothing supernatural about ghosts. They are part of the world in which we live, and they follow laws which we are beginning to understand more fully as more and more research into the parapsychological continues to be done. It is our hope that this book will help people to understand the world of so-called spirits a little more fully, and help them also to face and deal with problems that occur far more frequently than is generally believed.

Robin Skelton

Introduction: Starting Out

'I Think We Have A Ghost'

Sometimes it begins with a phone call, and sometimes with a not-quite-casual snatch of conversation at a social gathering. Sometimes the approach is direct, but not very often. Usually the subject is circled around for a little while before it is properly broached. Hardly anyone comes out with it straight away and says, 'My house is haunted. Can you do something about it?' Frequently they say, with some embarrassment, 'I think we have a ghost.'

The trouble is that most people are unwilling to admit that something might be sufficiently wrong to deserve attention. They don't like to admit that their home has a ghost, or ghosts, in residence. For one thing, it might pull down the value of their property, and for another it makes one's friends nervous. Sometimes, too, people do not understand the situation at all. They feel depressed in the house, although it is most comfortable, full of cherished possessions, and they have no worries. Yet they feel terribly depressed, especially in the bedroom, it may be, or the basement. One person will say that there is something wrong with the wiring, for the lights keep flickering, and the doorbell rings when nobody is there. The wiring has been inspected and there's nothing wrong with it. Do you suppose that …? Another person may say that his wife has begun to see and feel things. He's very worried about her. He doesn't think she's losing her mind, but it is very worrying. Do you imagine that, just possibly …? Some people tell the story as if it were a joke, but the humour is strained, and the eyes are anxious.

'I keep hearing this crying,' someone will say. 'I hear it almost every night. I thought it was just me, that I was imagining it, but then someone else heard it too.' Visible spectres are rarer, and more puzzling, for they do not look like Marley's ghost in *A Christmas Carol*, and they don't wear bed sheets and are not transparent. Most of the time they look exactly like living beings, like intruders, but then they disappear, suddenly. As one plaintive person said to me, 'It's all a bit unnerving.'

Faced with these harassed people, one must first of all explain that there is nothing terribly unusual about their experiences. They happen all the time and are entirely natural phenomena. We know that everything on earth has an energy field, and sometimes patches of energy are left around by people who have died, or even by living people. It is, one must say comfortingly, a bit like an echo that goes on being repeated after the original sound has been made. The spectres, the visible ghosts, occur when the energy field creates a kind of hologram; the place has been imprinted with a sort of photograph that comes into view from time to time, often when there's a particular atmospheric condition. One says all these things, and one talks of 'grounding' the energy. It is all, one says, quite simple really. There is no need to be afraid. A ghost cannot do anybody any actual physical harm. It may be a nuisance, a distraction, but it cannot hurt.

This is, of course, not entirely true, for phenomena of this kind do cause depressions and nervous storms, and these may have debilitating effects and can lead to people becoming accident-prone or even, one must face it, suicidal. It is, however, important to persuade people to look upon their ghosts as nuisances rather than threats, and as nuisances that can be got rid of without too much difficulty. Fear is more dangerous than any ghost. One must intimate that it is probably a very simple problem.

It may not be a simple problem, unfortunately. It may be quite a tricky one and require a good deal of investigation and a considerable amount of work. As one sets out to visit the affected house and its troubled inhabitants, one must keep an open mind and be prepared for almost anything. To begin with, one does not know exactly what kind of ghost or haunting one is facing.

Types of Ghosts

It is not generally appreciated that the phenomena we call ghosts come in a number of different guises and have a variety of causes. One kind is simply the consequence of the energy field of a house being disturbed or distorted. A house that has been left empty for a long time, for example, often suffers from a kind of psychic malnutrition. It was built to house people, to be sustained by their energies, their thoughts and emotions, and if deprived of these it may develop a terrible insecurity, a kind of hunger that drains the new owners of energy and depresses them, or troubles them with insomnia and makes them accident-prone. Such houses are easily comforted and cleansed.

Some houses are troubled by imprints of events that have happened there. The passions and anxieties of previous owners have left an energy field behind them, have caused psychic echoes. Sometimes these energy fields are very strong indeed and cause cold patches in one or more of the rooms of the house. Not infrequently one can find a cold patch about the area of a kitchen table and can walk into it and out of it again as if one were passing through an invisible fridge. The field is feeding upon people's energy, lessening their body heat. This temperature-loss is not imaginary but real, as the use of a thermometer will reveal.

What one might call the orthodox ghost is, of course, the spirit of someone who has died. This person has failed, somehow, to make a complete departure from this phase of life into the next one, and is confused. He or she is convinced that nothing much has changed and cannot understand why no attention is being received. This spirit or entity demands attention and goes about getting it by disturbing the electricity in the house, switching lights on and off, ringing door bells. It may open and close doors. It may move objects from one place to another. This kind of ghost has to have the situation explained to it, and be told, firmly but kindly, that it really belongs elsewhere and must leave. Often such spirits are attached to particular objects of which they were very fond in their earthly life, and it is these that keep them hanging around.

Some spirits that remain in residence after their physical presence has departed are not, however, the spirits of dead people at all. People can leave their presence behind them when they move to another house in another place. Sometimes a person in a nursing-home will leave his or her spirit behind, or even send it from the new house to the old home. Not infrequently this will happen when a person is dying and thinking of saying goodbye to someone far away. At the point of death or, usually, a little while afterwards, this person will appear to the loved one, quite briefly, and then vanish. The old term for this kind of ghost was 'a fetch'.

The earth itself, the land on which a house is built, may also cause phenomena of this kind. A house built on land which has been used for religious ceremonies, or for other high-energy activities, is likely to retain the imprint of these. We know of several Canadian houses that have been disturbed by echoes of Indian ceremonies of the past, for example. Sometimes, too, a house built over an underground stream will be affected, for running water is a great conductor of psychic energy fields. It seems also that electricity stations, or patches of rock that have developed radio-activity from the natural processes of decay, provide a good gathering-place for ghosts.

I say 'gathering-place' deliberately, for, odd though it may appear, ghosts are gregarious. I do not mean that they meet for parties or coffee-mornings in the attic or hold seminars in the cellar. I mean that if a place has one ghost it is quite likely to have one or two more. Sometimes a house will have a whole host of them, and these are difficult houses to deal with, for each presence may require a different approach.

The earth's own energy field may also be responsible for a special kind of ghostly activity. It may form entities that may reasonably be called 'spirits', for they function as individual entities. They are usually termed 'elementals' and are inclined to be mischievous. An energy field not derived from a human personality has no sense of right or wrong. It is pure energy, and some of the activities that elementals perform are very tiresome indeed; one elemental we came across had a habit of causing the mail to disappear, for example.

Another kind of ghost is not a ghost proper but an energy field that has been placed in a particular object and initially for a purpose. A statue or figure that has been used in religious ritual will often contain an energy field that continues to send out its power long after it has been relegated to the shelves of an antique shop or the mantelpiece of a collector. We know one Oriental figure that made life really miserable for the family that owned it, and a Polynesian carving that has to be kept happy with a vase of flowers beside it if it is not to cause mischief. It must be realized that any object that has been subjected to a force field of strong emotions is likely to retain that field, as if it were a piece of metal that had been magnetized. This is why second-hand rings and necklaces should be treated with circumspection; one does not know exactly what forces they are carrying.

Sometimes it is not a place or object that is inhabited by a spiritual, or psychic, force but a person. The term commonly used for this is 'possession', but this sounds as if the person is wholly controlled by an alien spirit, which is rarely the case. I myself prefer to think of the possessing spirit as a kind of lodger, a tiresome lodger with very strong views. The task of the person called in to help the house-owner is one of eviction.

Assessing the Problem

It is easy to understand that when one is approached by someone who says nervously that a house seems to be haunted, one does not know exactly what one is up against. Therefore it is necessary, boy-scout like, to 'be prepared' and so visit the place with an open mind and with enough equipment to deal with any eventuality.

The first step is, however, to talk and to wander round the house and feel it out. A long talk is usually necessary. It is a bit like a confession. The whole picture emerges only slowly. Quite frequently people will not mention something because they don't think it is relevant, because it does not fit in with what they think of as ghostly activity. They may dismiss the dog's disinclination to go into their daughter's bedroom as too trivial to mention, or because they have decided that the dog does not like the girl's perfume. They may dismiss disappearing objects as the consequence of absent-mindedness on their part. They may even blame oddities of the telephone upon the telephone company. They will provide rational explanations for everything they can, and they will sometimes look a little dubious when one suggests that an inability to breathe comfortably in the basement may be due to something other than an allergy to wood dust. One can see them thinking that one is a little crazy and inclined to think of everything that happens in terms of the supernatural.

I sometimes think that the word 'supernatural' should be excised from the dictionary. Hauntings and ghosts are not supernatural at all; they are a part of the natural world in which we live, and they are as subject to natural laws as anything else. Many things we now take for granted as natural phenomena were once considered supernatural – magnetism, for example, and even fire. We now accept telepathy as natural, and auras have been made respectable by the discovery of Kirlian photography. Our difficulty with ghosts is that, while we know how to deal with the majority of them, and while we can explain them to a degree, we cannot yet formulate the laws that are in operation in a fashion that satisfies the sceptical.

Moreover, not everyone is sensitive to this kind of phenomenon. In a given family it is frequent for one person to be troubled, and this leads sometimes to family dissension. And there still are a great many people who assert roundly that they do not believe in ghosts. For us this is rather like saying one does not believe in air. We are surrounded by energies, and for the most part we do not choose to notice them particularly or think about them. We feel uncomfortable or happy in this place or that; we prefer this room to that room; we have one piece of jewellery that we love wearing and one we wear rarely, though it may be more valuable or more attractive than the other. We pick up the 'vibrations' of everything around us, just as we breathe the air, without thought and automatically. It is only when the air is filled with smoke, or polluted, or heavy with perfume, that we take note of it and complain. Similarly, it is only when the energy fields with which we live become distinctly noticeable that we are troubled and call for help.

The job of the ghost-hunter, or exorcist, is to help people clear the air and make breathing once again easy, casual, unconstrained.

Equipment for the Hunt and for the Rite

Medical doctors carry a selection of instruments and medicaments to those privileged people on whom they make house-calls. Ghost-hunters do the same, and they furnish themselves with a number of objects which may be of use, first in diagnosing exactly what is wrong, and secondly in improving the situation. Were we to make a shopping-list for a beginning ghost-hunter, it would be as follows. (Many of the implements are supplies are also essential to the rite of exorcism given in the Appendix.)

The first thing you really need is a cane or wand, preferably black, with either a silver or a white handle. This is to be used for drawing circles when these prove to be necessary, for focusing upon disturbed areas and also for measuring distances. One does not want to crawl around with a tape-measure when visiting a haunted house in which a chair or table has moved unaccountably; it is easier and less obtrusive to work in terms of cane-lengths.

The next thing required is some sort of carrying-case. An old-fashioned make-up case, of the kind that can easily be found in a flea-market, would be perfect. Jean's is of black leather with a handle, and it has a lot of little pockets in it so that different items can be carried easily without confusion, and in the lid is a mirror which, she maintains, not wholly seriously, can be invaluable if she should run into a vampire, as vampires are supposed to produce no reflection in a mirror, and mirrors are therefore useful in detecting them.

The first object you should place in your case is protection oil. This can be bought in any occult supplies shop under that name, or you can use any oil that you personally feel to be right and that feels good. You can, of course, make your own if you wish. One recipe for protection oil suggests beginning with mineral or sesame seed oil, adding a teaspoon of a prepared mixture of bergamot, vervain, eyebright, flax and basil. Also put in it jade, real pearls or a protective talisman that you wear frequently. Let this soak on a windowsill for twenty-eight days, and then strain and bottle it. It should be applied to the third eye, the pineal gland situated one inch above the bridge of the nose, the hollow at the base of the throat, and the palms of the hands. If the house you are visiting feels particularly malevolent, it is wise to anoint everyone present.

If you feel it necessary, you may chant a spell while preparing or bottling the oil. One such traditional chant is: 'With this oil I purify, protect and renew my purpose, that all deeds performed by me shall be for the good of all.'

Sea-salt should also be placed in the case. Sea-salt is the spiritual equivalent of iodine, dettol or lysol; it disinfects and purifies whatever it touches, and should be kept in glass or china jars, never in metal or plastic containers. It can be bought at any health food store. Salt does not need to be exorcized, but it should be briefly blessed with such words as: 'Creature of Salt, I bless you, that you may help me in my work.' This blessing, once given, lasts for ever and does not need to be renewed on every occasion.

Incense is essential equipment. It can take many forms – powder, sticks or cones. Jean prefers loose incense for exorcisms. Incense can be bought in occult supply stores, and sticks of it are easily found in Oriental gift shops. It is wise to use frankincense or sandalwood. Really sweet incenses, such as musk and saffron, and incenses of a fruity kind are to be avoided, as they do not have a cleansing quality. Loose incense is burned on discs of soft charcoal and can be obtained at any religious supply shop. Stick incense is used in exorcizing houses, buildings or objects. It should be lit at the front door and carried around so that its fumes touch all the outside walls of the house, as we will see later in the Appendix.

If proper incense is not available, a small charcoal briquette can be broken up into a container (you must be very sure that the container is metal and that it rests upon a heavy coaster or asbestos pad), then you can sprinkle the briquette with cinnamon or cloves; an even simpler trick is to use a cup of warm water sprinkled with spices and citrus peels. Even an orange or apple cut in half and sprinkled with spices can be used instead of incense.

(The general principle is that, while it is preferable to use the conventional implements and supplies, in an emergency one can use anything that comes to hand and has the right symbolic significance. One would not wish to substitute Ribena for wine, or biscuits for bread, but at a pinch it could be done and would serve.)

Candles form an important part of many ceremonies and rituals. Each time we burn a candle we perform an act of sacrifice. The sacrifice consists of giving up, consuming or killing something of value for the sake of someone or something else, or in order to achieve a purpose. The word 'sacrifice' derives from two Latin words, *sacra*, meaning holy, and *facere*, make; to sacrifice something is to make it holy or to make it a spiritual or psychic force, to redirect its energy by transforming it.

The burning of incense or of a candle is perhaps the easiest and most potent sacrifice. It is a deliberate act that has an immediate result. We can smell or see the incense or the flame. We burn a candle to make a room more romantic, to make our table look hospitable, to make an occasion festive or sometimes even just to chase the dark away.

Entities are attracted to light and to scent, and a candle flame will respond to human thought. Candles used in ceremonies should never be blown out, because this disperses the energy. They must be put out deliberately, with a pinch of the fingers or with a candle-snuffer, and with the words, 'Grateful thanks be to you, O creature of fire and light', or allowed to go out naturally on their own.

The colours of the candles are important. They affect the emotional atmosphere, the energy field of the place in which they are lit. In exorcism they should be chosen to appeal to the nature and character of the entity one commands to appear. This entity may take on a human shape; it may appear as a shadow or a thickening of the atmosphere in the room, but sometimes it can be attracted to the light of a candle and drawn into it. Several candles are used during an exorcism, in case more than one entity is involved. In any haunting it is not uncommon for there to be a major presence and one or two minor ones. One might almost call them hangers-on; when the main entity has left, they either leave also or cease to have any effective energy.

The candles used in rituals should not be scented, for the perfume adds another and often irrelevant dimension to the proceedings. Most ceremonies include two or four white or cream candles. If the ceremony involves a balancing of energies, sometimes one white candle and one black are used.

Red or orange candles are rarely used in an exorcism. Red is the colour of immense vitality, even rage, anger, and while red candles may be appropriate for a revitalizing ritual they are not useful for exorcism unless the entity commanded to appear is a very angry one indeed. Orange is also a vitalizing colour. Jean has used orange candles to banish anxiety, as on one occasion when a dentist's office had been taken over by a bookshop, and customers proved disinclined to linger there. When orange candles had dispelled the anxiety in the place, she brought in mellow-coloured candles to provide an atmosphere of comfort and security, pale yellow for intellect, coral pink for sentiment, some blue candles for adventurous and outdoor feeling, and a light spring-green candle for youthful vitality and promise. In this way she was creating an atmosphere that would be acceptable to people of many temperaments.

Other colours reflect and create other moods and qualities. A true green provides balance, a green-blue suggests cleansing and health, a yellow green implies envy, and blue is decisive, creative and logical. Violet is rarely used in rituals, for it is fixed, uncompromising and sometimes suggests a touch of madness. Black candles may be used to burn away negative energies. If you move into a house which feels uncomfortable, you might do well to burn a black candle or candles in the basement for twenty-four hours. Black absorbs and consumes. White candles or cream candles with a natural bone colour are used most frequently; they reflect whatever is good, cleansing, purifying, happy, loving, caring.

Candles for an exorcism are chosen to reflect the apparent character and mood of the disturbing entity. Grey would be appropriate for earth-bound, boring, routine people. It is rarely used. Dark grey is for people who are bored and frustrated. Brown is almost never used in a ritual, as it is grounding and stabilizing. Rose is for romantic, teenage, flirtatious personalities. Mauve is suitable for an older woman, and also for a frivolous woman who lives in a dream world, which is why a mauve candle was used for the exorcism in St David Street described in Chapter 3.

Water is also needed. It should not be tap water, as this is now so polluted with algae or chlorine or metals from lead or copper pipes that it is no longer pure. Water from a sacred spring or stream could be used, or from some place that you intuitively feel is right. Distilled and purified water lacks vitality, and so if Jean uses it she usually adds about an ounce of good sparkling mineral water, such as Perrier, to put some life back into it.

The water should be kept in a glass bottle or china jar and should be exorcized and blessed with a formula such as: 'Creature of water, I exorcize thee in the names of Goodness and Mercy, that thou shalt cast out from thee all the impurities and phantoms of this or other worlds, and this I ask in the names of Goodness and Mercy.'

Obviously, you should always carry a notebook. It is important to write down descriptions of people and of objects, and to make maps of the house and of the arrangement of the contents of the rooms, as well as to keep a good running record of what you do. A tape recorder can be used to record the interview with the householders as an addition to your notes. A tape recorder may also be left running in an empty room with a piece of masking tape over the microphone, or with the microphone disconnected. Frequently a tape recorder will pick up sounds, or even the voices, of entities. Tape recorders must not be relied upon as the only way of recording information, however, for the energy fields sometimes make them misfunction.

A camera can also be valuable, though it is quite common for it also to fail to function. The camera should be loaded with a brand-new film before you enter the house, and when the film is developed, the negatives should be scrutinized as carefully as the prints. Things to look for are: spots of light, bars of light, patches that are reflecting or shiny, shadows where no shadows should be, double exposures and images which were not seen by the naked eye. Photographs or negatives will sometimes show images of people who were not physically present. Polaroid cameras are exceptionally useful, as the photograph can be checked on the spot and there is no danger of accidental double-exposure. Sometimes the camera itself is affected. Jean once used a polaroid camera that appeared to be haunted. A photograph of a family in Victoria showed members of the family who were at that time in Nevada. Every picture that was taken imposed itself upon the picture following, until a picture was taken of a cathedral, after which normality returned.

A compass is also useful but, like the camera and the tape recorder, it is quite likely to misfunction. You are, after all, dealing with energy fields, and these can affect anything magnetized.

A drum is an excellent tool. If you drum gently and regularly in a room, it can focus the energies and attract the attention of whatever entities are present.

You may wish to take some protective talismans with you. These should be ones to which you have a strong attachment.

An ordinary brown paper bag should also be included in your

kit. If there is an object in the house that you wish to take away, it is better to take it away in a brown paper bag than in your hand, or unwrapped. Plastic is no good, but you could wrap the object in a piece of silk if you so wished.

Onions are useful for diagnostic purposes. Take an onion and cut it into quarters. Then place one quarter in each corner of the room and leave it there for not less than twenty-four hours. If there is something wrong about the room, if some entity is present, one or more of the quarters will become slimy instead of drying up normally as one would expect. Garlic, which has sometimes been considered useful in operations of this kind, is of no value in other than flower form.

Divining-rods should be included in the kit. These days expensive divining-rods can be bought in many occult supply shops, but the cheapest, the easiest to make and the most useful is made of a welding-rod turned at a ninety-degree angle, fitted into the sleeve of a thin copper pipe. Metal coat-hangers also make excellent divining-rods. These can pick up the energy from ghosts.

A pendulum is useful. It may be made of a ring, a button, a darning needle or a crystal on a strong thread or cord of natural fibre – linen, cotton, wool, not polyester. One can hold the pendulum over a piece of broken pottery, or a cold spot in the house, or even some suspect object. You should notice whether it swings deosil (clockwise) or widdershins (anti-clockwise). If it moves only back and forth, notice in what direction its path lies; this may direct you to a focal point of energy. If it moves in one direction, then a second, and then a third, the object over which it is swinging is to be regarded as holy or extremely powerful. You will get that powerful a reading from a crucifix, a Bible, a Torah or a deck of Tarot cards.

Tarot cards are, of course, an excellent tool, as they can be used to do a reading on a situation, an object or a house, as well as for a person involved in the situation that is being investigated.

A mini-maxi thermometer should also be carried. These can be bought in nurseries and garden stores; they are constructed to measure the lowest temperature and the highest temperature, and the indicators remain in place. This is enormously important in investigating cold spots. Jean remembers using the thermometer on one cold spot and finding that the temperature was six degrees lower in one place than in another only a foot away; this was in the middle of a room, and there were no open windows or doors or heating-ducts to affect the temperature.

A chalice or cup should also be placed in the case. If it is of metal, you must be careful to clean it and dry it after it has been used, or it will corrode.

A piece of chalk is also necessary. This is used to mark circles around chairs or other pieces of furniture so that it can be seen if they have moved during an exorcism or perhaps during the night. Chalk can also be used to draw circles, and to make symbols of protection in places where this seems advisable. A five-pointed star can be drawn in chalk above or before any opening such as a door, fireplace or heating-duct. Symbols or signs may also be drawn to attract entities, either to make them appear or to confine them in one area.

A small handbell is also useful. It can be used to begin and end ceremonies, or simply to attract energy.

Coloured sand can also be helpful. It may be used instead of chalk to make circles, as one does not wish to leave permanent marks on a carpet, and sand can easily be vacuumed up after a ceremony is over. Coloured sand can also be laid in stripes on a platter or bowl, and then gently agitated or shaken, when it may form an image which will help you to decide what kind of entity is in the house.

Jean once dealt with a haunted house in which there were a great many East Indian artefacts, and it was difficult to determine which of these was the focal-point of the energy which was causing trouble. Blue and grey and orange sand was laid on a silver tray in stripes and then agitated. The tray was then tapped three times by the owner of the house, and the image of an elephant was formed. Jean examined all the artefacts which presented images of elephants and found one which had had a curse placed upon it. Without the assistance of the sand, it would have taken hours or even days to examine all the artefacts in the room.

Necessary Research

Before any of these implements are used, however, it is important to do as much research as possible on the house itself, to discover who has owned it and, even more importantly, who has lived, or died, in it. This can be managed by utilizing the city directory in the local library. It is as well, also, to discover what one can of the history of the land upon which the house was built, and sometimes the name and nature of the architects and builders may be significant. One should also do one's best to learn something of the background of the present householders; it is not unknown for a householder to have actually brought the disturbing entity into the house. The more one learns about everything to do with the place, the more likely one is to succeed in clearing up the disturbances.

The First Visit

Once the initial interview and research are over, it is important to arrive at the house to be investigated at an appropriate time. If the ghost has a way of appearing at a certain hour, arrive a couple of hours earlier. The householders should be asked to stay outside as you investigate, so that their vibrations do not confuse the situation; indeed, it is often wise to arrange for them to be wholly absent and to leave the key for you under the mat, or lend you a duplicate.

Once inside the house, the first thing to do is to breathe in the atmosphere, moving gently and undramatically from place to place – even, from time to time, talking to the house. Take careful note of how your breathing sounds. Often the house itself seems to breathe. Sometimes it will hiss, and sometimes it will sigh; sometimes you will feel that it is gasping. Note all your reactions, open yourself to the way the house touches your feelings, your emotions and what comes into your mind.

However trivial these tiny thoughts and fantasies may be – snatches of a song, small pictures, hints of perfume – remember them, for they are all clues. This wandering may seem far from energetic, but you are in fact using a great deal of energy, and it is wise to drink a fair amount of water or lemonade before beginning work, for ghost-hunting tends to cause dehydration.

Take notes of everything you perceive, and, in talking to the household, note the usual rhythm of their days, the times at which they eat or watch television, go out or come in. Take note also of the weather; there may well be a correlation between the weather and the hauntings. Rainy evenings are particularly inclined to suffer from ghostly visitations. Also consider the phases of the moon; some phenomena occur only when the moon is in a particular phase, or when there is no moon at all. Some ghosts, too, are seasonal and come into action only in springtime or autumn, or even during a particular month or on a particular day. One cannot know just how important many of these apparently trivial details may be.

Another matter to bear in mind is the cultural context in which the trouble originated. You must tackle the entity in terms it can understand; you must find common ground. For example, if the offending entity is Coast Indian, you should make use of symbolism deriving from that culture; if the influence is African, you should use fetishes made out of feathers and bones and bring fruits of an appropriate kind. If the entity is well educated, the exorcism must be conducted with careful attention to correct grammatical usage. It is not necessary to dress up as an Indian or an African witch doctor, or a nineteenth-century schoolmaster; that would be absurd. You need only provide enough common ground for a meeting to be possible, and this can be done with very little trouble.

When visiting a haunted house, it is wise to take some antacid, as the work often causes acidity and heartburn. You should wear loose-fitting clothing in which you feel comfortable, and it should be dark-coloured, preferably black, for black absorbs energy and therefore increases perception, whereas white reflects energy and consequently limits sensitivity. It is interesting to note that black has always been regarded as the colour of wisdom.

A clean linen handkerchief is a good idea also, because you may have to wipe away someone's tears. Emotions often become strained, for this is an important time. The tears are often tears of relief, for feelings and fears that had hitherto been regarded as too private or too absurd to be mentioned are now being taken seriously. The householder is being told, 'This is real. This is not your imagination. You are not insane. And we can help you.'

Some people, even though they have asked for help, are scared by the word 'exorcism'. They may have seen movies which make the whole process melodramatic and alarming, or they may feel that it is unwise to meddle with something they have been taught to regard as supernatural. Sometimes they will tell their stories and then refuse to have any exorcism performed, saying that, really, the ghost is not much trouble, so why should one bother? It is necessary to tell these people that it may not really be healthy to live in a house that is haunted; it can be, at least, debilitating.

Many houses can be 'cleaned' without any ceremonial ritual at all. Sometimes the householder can be advised to do a number of quite commonplace things to clear the matter up. Sometimes, however, the situation is complicated. In the pages that follow, we describe our experiences of some of the most complicated and some of the most simple hauntings with which we have dealt, either together or with other helpers, over the years. It has been, and remains, a fascinating pursuit and is constantly enlivened by surprises and confusions. It appears to be a rule that no investigation of a haunting ever goes entirely smoothly. There are cancellations of appointments, mislaid addresses, car failures and often comical contretemps. Ghost-hunting demands not only great care and sensitivity but also that one retain one's sense of humour. Indeed, some ghosts, can be banished by laughter.

1

The House on the Hill

It was the summer of 1978, and it all began, as so many ghost-hunts do, with a phone call to Jean. Could she pay a visit to a haunted house? The owners needed advice and help.

The only day available for the first visit, however, was Father's Day, which was a little inconvenient, as Jean and her friends all had husbands and children, and there were Father's Day parties to go to. Nevertheless, Jean and her two friends Cece and Betty set off in Jean's car. Jean usually takes companions on these adventures. It is as well to have several note-takers and observers; quite frequently no two people see or feel exactly the same things. Moreover, both Cece and Betty were fully trained mediums and efficient psychics and also very close friends. They had worked together a great deal and had always been good companions over the years. However, on the way out to the house they fought and argued constantly. Jean had never seen them have any kind of personality conflict before and was somewhat surprised.

She was less surprised at the difficulty they had in finding the house, for it is not unusual for the first visit to any haunted house to be delayed in one way or another. They drove past the house and couldn't find the driveway, which difficulty, Jean says, she always considers to be a good sign, because it means something is trying to prevent her from going there. Finally they found the house and drove up the serpentine 200-yard drive.

The building was halfway up a hill, a small, white,

comfortable-looking house, probably built in the late 1940s or early fifties, and certainly not anybody's idea of a haunted house. There were a good many trees around it, and a new addition had been built on the house at the back. There was a patch of level cleared ground where the car could be parked. There was no conventional garage, but there was an open-sided roofed structure beside the house which would hold as many as two cars and a truck. It was decorated with deer horns, and its primitive, rural appearance was quite out of keeping with the house itself. Somehow or other it felt uncomfortable, even ominous, though Jean did not, at that time, understand why.

The owners of the house, John and Margaret, were tall, thin and quite obviously British. There was an air of the meticulous about them, and they were very courteous and well-mannered. They were accompanied by a big old dog, woolly and black, a cross-breed. It moved very slowly and had a lump on its back which was caused by a growth which had appeared, Jean was told, only since its owners had acquired the house. Margaret was all too clearly in poor health (she had had a colostomy), and John appeared strained and nervous. Although they were working on the house, as they did most weekends, and were wearing casual clothes, they retained an air of elegance, and John had the look of a man who would not be inclined to get his finger-nails dirty. He seemed, indeed, a little remote from the ordinary hurly-burly of life, a man of sensibility who would take pleasure in beautiful things.

Jean asked John and Margaret to remain outside the house while she, Cece and Betty began their investigations. They didn't want to be distracted or have their concentration disturbed. In addition they did not want to be told what exactly had been happening in the house and what the trouble was, because they wished to get their own fresh impressions and not be influenced by information which might lead them to think along set lines or be prejudiced. Cece and Betty entered the house separately, one after the other, and walked through it. They were told to do anything they wished, and were required to keep careful, detailed notes of what they felt, what they saw and any hunches that came to them.

When they had thoroughly examined the house, the whole group met in the den for tea. The den was the additional room that had been built on the back of the house and had windows on three sides. John and Margaret called it 'the solar', which seemed a little pretentious, for 'solar' is a now obsolete word. In the eighteenth century it was an old word for an upper room or garret and is still in use only in country districts in the form 'sollar'. John and Margaret, presumably, derived it from 'solarium', which originally meant a terrace but which could mean a sun-room.

It was an unpleasant house. The walls seemed to be tilted; the floors seemed to move under one's feet so as almost to throw one off balance. The area near the front window was so depressing that Cece and Betty both wanted to cry. There were cold spots in a number of places; in the bedroom the patch of cold was particularly intense. They were afraid of the basement also; it was extremely unpleasant, and one small room, pleasingly panelled and furnished, was so appalling that all three investigators simply refused to enter it. One unfinished room directly below the dining-room was almost entirely filled by a big outcrop of rock. Its walls were roughly surfaced and there were shelves containing old bottles and miscellaneous junk. A door out of this room led to a smaller room originally used as a coal cellar.

After this first survey, everyone found it hard to describe the rooms precisely; their notes showed many differences, for each room appeared to change its shape and character for each observer. One saw a bed with a headboard, fully made up with sheets, blankets and pillowcases, and set against the wall, and yet, in actuality, the bed was in the middle of the room wrapped in plastic, just as it had been delivered from the store, and there was no headboard anywhere in the room.

Cece and Betty became very nervous and upset, and their personalities changed even more than they had during the drive in the car. Cece, who was normally shy and reticent, became loud-voiced and aggressive and began using four-letter words.

Betty tried to stop anyone else speaking; she constantly interrupted the conversation, and later said that it was only by a great effort of will that she prevented herself getting up from her seat and actually striking her friend.

As Cece and Betty described what they had seen and felt, John and Margaret were able to confirm almost everything they had perceived. They too had felt the terrible depression before the front window. They had experienced the cold spot in the bedroom and had suffered vertigo while walking down the hallway. They had felt as if the floor were moving underneath them. They had felt afraid of being pushed down the stairs to the basement. They had also felt that there was something very wrong with the shape of the bathroom. In addition, on entering the dining-room they would often find that a large potted plant had been freshly watered, although nobody had been in the house for a week. Furniture also was moved, so Jean taught them to draw chalk circles around the legs of the furniture before they left the house and also to spread about two feet of talcum powder or baby-powder in front of the doors. Invariably when they returned there would be no marks on the talcum but the furniture would have been moved, and always the one plant in the dining-room would have been freshly watered. One day a large rock had been placed in the flower pot. Oddly enough, immediately under the dining-room was the unfinished basement room containing the large rock outcrop.

They had also suffered a fear of something green looking in the windows of the solar; they referred to this as 'the green man'. On entering the solar they had felt a compulsion to go and stand in a corner and stare at the blank wall behind which the bathroom was situated. At the top of the basement stairs, too, they had felt panic and terror, and an unpleasant dirty feeling in the basement itself; this was so strong that they were unable to enter one small basement room. This feeling affected Jean so strongly that, she says, 'Although I am addicted to antiques, I was unable to enter and examine a very beautiful carved antique rocking-chair.' There were many such beautiful pieces in the house; its furnishings were lovely but the atmosphere was such that none of the three investigators felt that they would be able to stay in it alone for more than a few minutes.

Margaret was too unwell to deal with the labour involved in laying fires in a real fireplace, so the house had been provided with a beautiful brand-new brass electric fireplace. When they returned to the house the week after it had been installed, the brass was corroded and had turned green. It was returned to the manufacturer, who told them that someone had urinated on it.

As far as John and Margaret were concerned, the situation was desperately ironic. Many years earlier they had drawn up plans for their dream home, and this house was almost identical in every way to the one they had envisaged. They had bought it two years earlier, and immediately things began to go wrong. The basement flooded, which was strange, for the house was set high up on a hill. Admittedly there was a pool behind the house, but it was about 200 yards away and only eighteen feet by fifteen. Moreover, it had never caused any seepage, much less flooding, into the house previously, as the original bone-dry state of the basement revealed. It did not appear, either, to be fed by any stream, for it was muddy and stagnant and fringed with dead or dying vegetation.

After the house had been pumped out and the debris and the furniture which had been stored there had been burned because it was too mouldy to be renovated, the house was invaded by rats. These were exterminated; the exterminators said that the rats, afflicted by thirst, would go out to the pool at the back of the house and die there as soon as they had drunk. However, they did not leave the house; they climbed into the walls and died there, and the stench of decay filled the house.

Men were hired to work in the house, but something always happened to prevent them from coming. Margaret's health became worse because of the anxiety and stress, and John began to experience periods of tremendous weariness; when he struggled to overcome his lassitude and work, he frequently injured himself, falling because of carelessness or absurd accidents. They both became so depressed that eventually they did little and could only sit in the house, unable to work or to plan, and Margaret began to be afraid that she was losing her mind. When at last they phoned Jean and she agreed to help them, they began to feel a little hope, although that same evening, as they were eating their meal, Margaret suddenly huddled down in her chair, began to wring her hands and moaned in a voice completely unlike her own, 'They must not come, they must not come. Oh please don't let them come in the house!' Then she straightened up in her chair and continued the conversation as if nothing had happened. When John asked her why she had said, 'Don't let them come', she insisted that she had said no such thing.

Several times while telling the three visitors of their adventures in the house Margaret burst into tears. Her relief and John's when Jean told them that they believed they could be helped was overwhelming. Apart entirely from the stress and anxiety the hauntings were causing them, they were also finding it a financial burden to keep up two houses, for they were only visiting the house on the hill at weekends and were living in another house the remainder of the time.

Taking all this into account, and especially Margaret's health, Jean told them that the best course of action would be to leave the house entirely and sell it. They asked for an alternative solution, and Jean told them that they could fight, and would certainly win, but that the emotional strain would be enormous, and she did not think that Margaret was strong enough. They asked her what could happen, and she told them that the feeling of loneliness and despair could become so strong that Margaret could no longer fight it and that she could slide into a depression from which she would never be able to recover. She told them that, if they wished, after thinking it over, she and her friends would be prepared to perform an exorcism ceremony but that the results could be dangerous to everyone involved, as well as cause damage to the house.

As soon as this had been said, the atmosphere of the house became deadly cold; air billowed up from between the floorboards; the lights began to flicker off and on; the windows creaked and a drumming began from underneath the floor.

Margaret lost consciousness for a few seconds in a swoon. Jean told them to leave everything and get out of the house. Outside it was a sunny June day, blue-skied and warm, and yet in the house it felt as if a storm was raging outside; the house creaked and moaned as if it was being attacked by a high wind, and there was a feeling of oppression. The drumming beneath the floor seemed halfway between the sound of heartbeats and the sound of breathing; it had begun slowly and picked up speed gradually; the vibration could be felt in the feet, and it was felt by everybody present, so that it was hard to dismiss it as a purely psychic phenomenon; all agreed that it was a real physical vibration.

John and Margaret insisted that they must do a little packing before they could leave the house. The intensity of the cold and the other phenomena had convinced them that they should go. Jean and her two friends ran out to their car to drive off in what Jean calls a 'cowardly' manner, but once they were outside, their fear abated, and so they waited while John and Margaret rinsed plates and emptied the fridge and put the contents in boxes to take away to their other house. Cece, Jean and Betty watched them bring the boxes out to their car, a shiny black Oldsmobile that looked as if it had only just been bought. As they watched, the catch of the boot disengaged itself, and the lid lifted before anyone had touched it. When John stooped over it to put a box in the boot, the lid slammed down and missed his head by inches.

There was no physical explanation. There was no wind. 'It was', Jean says, 'just malevolent.' Afterwards she and her friends examined the car and they could not make the lid fall in that fashion by hitting it, or banging it, or leaning on it. All three of the investigators kept notes, and all three recorded that John walked out of the basement door carrying a huge coil of rope over his arm and placed the rope in the big car port. The following week, when all five people were together again going over these notes, John insisted that this had never happened.

The three investigators drove home, and for the next seven days they led a somewhat troubled existence. Anything that could possibly go wrong, did. Jean arrived home to find unexpected company who refused an invitation to stay for dinner, but neither did they leave, so that her husband's meal had to be irritatingly delayed. While cooking pork chops, she dumped a whole jar of dill pickles, including juice, into the pan, in a fit of absent-mindedness. On Monday, after she had phoned John and Margaret, a bead curtain over some french doors in an archway leading off her living-room became agitated. One strand of the beads, and one strand only, began slowly to swing and then swung faster and faster until it was whipping about like the tail of an angry cat. The remainder of the curtain was entirely still.

Cece and Betty also had their problems. The three colleagues usually met on a Tuesday, but this had to be cancelled, and so they met on a Wednesday instead. As they began their usual meditation session, there was a huge thump on the door, as if, Jean says, 'an enormous animal had jumped against it'. There was no animal outside. As they settled down again, more thumps were heard on the door, and then there were a series of thumps all down the side of the building, a series of raps as if someone were beating the whole length of it with something like a baseball bat. This building was a garage that Jean's husband had built her at the back of the house for her meetings with her friends and students so that they would be safe from interruptions and phone calls. On the right-hand side of this building, and attached to it, was an enormous greenhouse, so that there was no way anyone could actually get at the wall in order to rap upon it. Jean and her friends left the building and went into the house proper, where it was decided that a seance at John and Margaret's was necessary in order to sort out exactly what was causing the happenings in the house on the hill.

Jean visited the couple to explain why she felt this to be a good idea, and to make arrangements. Because she could find no baby-sitter, she took her young son Kord, then not quite five years old, along with her, as well as her 16-year-old daughter, Tara, who was already experienced in these matters and therefore a valuable assistant.

While Jean was giving her explanation, and as they were all drinking tea out of elegant bone-china cups, a drumming noise began. It was as if the house itself were pulsing and breathing, and the vibration was so strong that it could be felt in the feet of everyone present. Then, as they watched, a silver-framed photograph lifted itself from a three-foot-high bookcase against one wall, made two complete somersaults in the air and landed on the floor at the other side of the room. Kord very carefully set down his cup and saucer and with one bound landed in his sister's lap with his arms around her neck, absolutely white-faced.

It was decided to hold the seance on the following Tuesday evening in the solar. An experienced medium, Judith Johnson, who had been away on vacation, had now returned, and she brought Mario, who is not only a sceptic but knows a great deal about recording-equipment. They met in the den and placed a tape recorder on a small table, with a heavy plastic place-mat beneath it to protect the polished surface. The table stood beneath the window where the green face had been seen looking in. The solar was carpeted wall to wall with a pale blue rug, and a card table was set up in the centre of the room with four folding chairs. John and Margaret sat on chairs near the door, their old dog at their feet. Cece, Judith, Betty and Mario sat at the table, forming a circle by linking their hands, right hand upon left. The circle should not be broken while the seance was in progress, or the person speaking in trance would become disorientated and distressed to the point of having severe headaches.

Jean sat beside the tape recorder, which had been loaded with a brand-new tape. When buying it, she had asked the sales clerk if she would watch her (Jean) wrap up the tape and seal it with sealing wax and then initial the package to certify that the tape was indeed new and untouched. The sales clerk became extremely uneasy and refused. On testing the tape for voice-level, difficulties occurred. First the machine would not work at all, and then it played back a great deal of static, and the sounds of a large, noisy party. After that it behaved itself and worked satisfactorily.

Cece was the first of the four around the table to speak, and she saw clairvoyantly a building which she described. John and

Margaret became extremely upset. Margaret turned her head towards Jean and screamed, 'Violator! Violator! Leave it alone! You are interfering! You are not wanted here!' She continued to shout, and her body slumped sideways, her neck twisted and she peered up at Jean.

Judith became upset and asked the company, 'Please send him away.' Cece appeared to have taken on a male character, and as she sat at the table her neck twisted to one side, but she continued to talk in trance, as everyone else went on shouting at each other. At last Cece fell silent, straightened up and became herself again, though she complained of a sore neck for the rest of the evening.

John and Margaret explained that the house she had seen was their other property, and it had been lived in by an old Swedish man who had built it and who later committed suicide by hanging himself in the barn. They felt that the twisted neck episode was therefore connected with the house in which they were now living, rather than the house on the hill.

Margaret then began to tell the company of the things she herself was perceiving clairvoyantly, and it became apparent that she was an accomplished medium. This was new information. Upon being challenged, Margaret admitted that she was a medium but had not worked for many years because of her poor health. She had worked in the Marylebone seances in Britain in the early forties, and her job as a teenager had been to contact the spirits of young airmen and sailors who had been killed and give them safe passage to the other world. This made Jean feel rather uncomfortable. If she was that powerful, why was she not taking care of the ghosts herself? Margaret insisted that it was because of her health and its problems.

So far the seance had been taking place in the dark, but when it came Betty's turn to speak, Margaret turned on the light and then, after a few moments, reluctantly turned it off again. The blackness became intense, almost unreal; everybody commented upon it. John assured the company that in a few seconds they would be able to see, but in fact the blackness increased and remained appallingly intense for the next twenty-three minutes.

It was so dark that one could not see across the table, and it became difficult for any of the participants to enter into a state of trance.

During this time Judith once again became extremely upset and began to cry, and the circle was broken for the first time during the seance. Betty said that she felt as if her back had been broken, and the pain continued for over a week.

The lights were turned on and Jean began to bait the ghost by making fun of it. It responded by making the lights blink, sometimes making them go on and off five or six times in rapid succession, and always in response to a question. Margaret interpreted in terms of what she herself picked up clairvoyantly. At this point everyone heard the sound of a heavy engine.

During a seance held a few days later, Jean and her friends contacted the spirit of a sailor who claimed to have had a homosexual relationship with an earlier owner of the house on the hill and said that when the other naval officers found out about this relationship he was transferred to another ship. There, after only three or four weeks, the boiler-room blew up and he died, breathing boiling oil. Such a ship accident had in fact occurred, but there is no certainty as to whether the rest of the story was real or imagined. It was possible that this particular spirit had been brought there by Margaret and was that of one of the young sailors she had contacted during her Marylebone seances, possibly one for whom she had felt an attraction.

As the investigators prepared to leave, they picked up the tape recorder and, underneath the thick plastic mat that had been put on the table to protect it, discovered five long, deep scratches. They looked as if they had been made by fingernails. Jean put her hand on the marks, but it was too small to fit them. John and Mario then tried, but their hands were also too small. As they folded up the card table and the chairs, they saw that the blue carpet was marked by a nine-foot circle of greasy dirt, splashed with drops of water. The front of Jean's robe was also covered in a sort of silvery grease, even though it had been freshly laundered before the visit, and the rest of the house contained nothing greasy on which she might have leaned. This was the first time the silver grease appeared, but after that it appeared on almost every visit the group made to the house. Smears of it were found on books as well as on clothes.

Jean did not play the tape of the seance back that evening. She left it until the next morning, as she felt they had all been stretched to their limits already. When she turned the tape recorder on, however, she found she had a recording of the local radio station, CKNW: she had recorded a complete evening's broadcast, including time-checks and weather reports. There had been no radios or television sets in the house, and the tape recorder itself had no radio.

The spirit of the sailor which appeared to have been responsible for these phenomena had, they decided, attached himself to Margaret because of her abilities as a medium, and also, they felt, because he took delight in making her use four-letter words which she, a particularly elegant and reticent woman, would never use in public normally.

At a later seance at Jean's house Margaret went into her trance and began to swear and curse and use foul language in a very husky male voice. She was roused almost immediately, as it could have been damaging to her health. When that seance ended, both Jean's friend Priscilla Bethel and Tara, who had been sitting side by side, found their hands covered with an oil – not the silver grease but true oil. It was felt that the entity responsible was Margaret's sailor, who was her personal demon and not one attached to the house. Therefore it was decided that she must get rid of him herself, and Jean advised her to use her skills as a medium to contact him directly and to command him to leave her, and to complete his journey to the next plane. This she managed to accomplish in less than a week.

It was now decided that a full-scale exorcism was needed, and Jean and her friends worked together on constructing an exorcism ceremony that would be appropriate in terms of their own beliefs but would not offend John and Margaret. On the day of the exorcism they prepared for the ceremony by fasting and by bathing in salt water, and they dressed themselves in loose, dark, non-restrictive clothing. When they arrived at the house, they found that John and Margaret had also dressed up for the occasion. They had chosen to wear some magnificent Indian jewellery of turquoise and silver. Cece and Betty also wore their own personal talismans, and Jean's daughter Tara, who had joined the group because she had herself taken part in a number of exorcisms, also wore talismans.

They arrived at dusk, taking with them sticks of incense, candles, salt, bread, wine, flowers and other equipment described in our Introduction. Cece and Betty were once again extremely nervous; the house appeared to have penetrated their very beings with its influence and even to have blocked out all they knew of such ceremonies. Jean, therefore, felt it necessary to take complete charge and to make whatever decisions had to be made during the proceedings.

The only illumination apart from the candle – to which the entities were summoned to receive their marching orders – was a large Spanish electric chandelier, which was controlled by a dimmer switch, turned to the halfway point.

The meditations of the previous week and the seance had led to the belief that there were several levels of haunting. One was an old lady, lonely and depressed, who was subject to sudden changes of personality, from silly childish giddiness to suicidal despair. She was situated mainly in the living-room. Another source of disturbance was a memory imprint of a teenager cut off from his friends and confined in the small barren basement room by a rather hypocritical father, so that he felt that he was imprisoned. In this room John and Margaret had found half-eaten tins of beans and sardines, and several pictures of naked women hidden in the walls. This teenager, they later discovered, was still alive but had left the imprint of his youthful emotions in the room.

John and Margaret had discovered that the former owner had been a naval officer who, during the period when the navy was being cut back, had been pensioned off, though only in his forties. It seemed that he decided to become a minister. Therefore, while living in this house he studied for the ministry. At the same time his wife became deeply involved with

Transcendental Meditation and taught meditation. They had a son who was going through the usual confusions and stresses of teenage years and was having a great deal of difficulty because neither of his parents appeared to have any notion of how to care for him or give him the companionship he needed. This was clearly the boy whose sexual fantasies were disturbing the basement.

A third ghost appeared to be the strongest of the three and was able to extend his influence outside the house. The den, or solar, was apparently his main domain, but he travelled freely throughout the house and seemed to be able to affect the lights. They later discovered that he could also affect tape recorders.

The ceremony proceeded. Cold spots were felt, but the atmosphere was not too unpleasant. All the spirits, or entities, in the house were called to draw nigh and submit to the exorcists' will. At that point the light went out. It did not flicker or waver. It was as if someone had turned off the chandelier. The light would not go on again until the dimmer had been turned up a full quarter. Jean took the salt-and-water mixture to the basement and told all evil and unhappy things to leave. She was alone and she spoke in a normal quiet tone of voice, but all the people upstairs, who were well acquainted with her voice, heard an argument in which three distinct voices shouted. When Jean returned, she sent Betty down to the basement, and Betty agreed with her that it was now free of all unpleasantness.

They next concentrated upon the old woman and told her that the house was no longer hers and that she must leave. At this, Margaret burst into tears and said, 'I must take one more look at this dear old house.' There was a loud sigh heard by everyone present, and the house felt suddenly empty, leaving them extremely drained. The candle flickered and went out, and a cold wind whirled around the room; it became very dark, and the air seemed too thick to see through. Margaret and Cece heard laughter coming from the hall and bedroom, and the more the group talked, the more intense became the cold and the louder the laughter. They realized that their physical and spiritual forces were too depleted to put up anything of a fight, and so they abandoned the struggle and left the house.

The exorcism had been held in the living-room, in front of a bookcase newly built in front of a set of mirrors which had been attached to the wall. Directly opposite to where they were standing, a mark began to appear on the back of the mirror as if someone was scraping the silvering away from the back. It grew about half an inch a week, until it was finally revealed as a very elaborate capital letter M.

Two Sundays later the group returned to the house, finished the exorcism, placed a protective spell upon the property and performed a ceremony at the pool on the hill behind the house. It was deep, black, muddy and lifeless; there were no insects or animals near it, and there were no water bugs of any kind. The vegetation around it was dead, and one tree slumped across it with its branches in the water. It was, Jean says emphatically, 'dead, lifeless, horrible', and she had thought that perhaps the green man who stared in the window of the solar had come from that place. Perhaps someone had been drowned there, she thought. An ancient spell to discover whether or not a drowning had taken place consists of floating a lit candle embedded in a loaf of bread upon the waters of the suspect pond or lake. If a person had been drowned there, the loaf should float for a little while and then turn over. Jean launched a candle and loaf, and the loaf floated round the pool for some time until it became waterlogged and sank. It did not turn over. Another ceremony was needed.

'One Sunday,' says Jean, 'we met at the pool. We were not able to make a complete circle around it because of the huge dead tree lying across it, so we made a semi-circle, a sort of horseshoe shape. First of all I exorcized the body of the water with the words:

' "I exorcize you, creature of water, that you will cast out all the impurities and uncleanliness of this world. I banish all evil by the power of Fire, Djinn, by the power of Earth, Gob, by the power of Air, Meralda, by the power of Water, Necka. Be all evil stopped in the name of Goodness and Mercy."

' "Into this water I make this sacrifice of silver, of parchment, of flowers, of salt, of bread and wine, that you shall be so nourished and claim no other sacrifice. This is my wish, and as I wish, so must it be".'

The sacrificial objects having been placed in the water, the group stood in meditation. Within twenty minutes a bird landed on a branch of the dead tree lying across the water, and almost immediately there were little water bugs on the water's surface. Within a week the apparently dead branches of the tree had sprouted green leaves. It was then August, and when September came, ducks visited the pool, which had come completely back to life.

Although John and Margaret had never been able to get workmen to the house, the morning after the exorcism was completed, a workman phoned them to say that he was suddenly free to do work for them and could indeed begin that very day. This was particularly strange, for John and Margaret had not contacted him for almost twelve months. The house now seemed very pleasant, and deer began to come down the hill and drink at the pool, which was now clear water, the mud having sunk to the bottom.

When the workmen started work on the old bathroom, they discovered a false wall which gave them eighteen extra inches of space. The false wall was directly behind the wall of the solar where John and Margaret had felt compelled to stand and stare. The passage behind the wall contained only the mummified body of one small mouse.

That seemed like the end of the matter, but such was not the case. The relief proved to be only temporary. Gradually everything began to happen again; the depression, the anxiety and the terror at the top of the stairs returned.

Jean and her friends began to wonder if the trouble might not be due to elementals or to the effects of underground water. Because of this Jean called on Mrs Priscilla Bethel, a water-diviner and quester, for help. When Priscilla approached the basement room containing the rock outcrop, John said, 'Be careful of the coal shed,' and just as she got to the door and was about to step in, the coldest and strongest wind that had ever hit her knocked her off balance. Tara, standing beside her, got the impression that she had been hit between the shoulder blades, because that was the part of her body that jerked forward. Priscilla, upon reflection and after more years of experience in investigation, now believes that there was probably radio activity there, due to decaying granite.

Nevertheless, Priscilla placed fresh, clean newspapers upon the rock and laid out her equipment. She found several 'hot spots' of energy in the house as she walked through it but could find no sign of polluted water or anything that could account for the movement of the furniture. When she went to pick up her dowsing-rods to go home, they were covered with the same silvery grease that had stained Jean's robe and the clothing of her friends.

Finally they all realized that they were almost back to square one. The house was still uninhabitable. Although the workmen turned up occasionally, nothing ever seemed to be achieved. One day, on arriving, Jean and her friends were told that an offer had been made for the house, and as much as John and Margaret wanted to keep it, in spite of the strain caused by their two mortgages, they decided that their only practical recourse was to give it up.

On arriving home, Jean found a telephone message from Priscilla, who told her that she had been doing some research on the house and the land on which it had been built. She had discovered that the first legal owner of the land area had been Sir Matthew Begbie, the first Chief Justice of British Columbia, who was popularly, though perhaps not justly, called 'The Hanging Judge'. He had owned the whole area around and used to ride out on horseback to shoot snipe. He spent a great deal of his time sitting upon the large outcrop of rock that now formed part of the basement of the house on the hill. There he would meditate, gazing off across the valley. At first Jean could think of no reason to connect Sir Matthew Begbie with the hauntings, and then she recalled the letter M that had scratched itself on the mirror behind the bookcase.

Jean and her friends were invited to visit the house one last time before it changed hands. Jean had recently met Carol Holland, who appeared to have the ability to take photographs which showed additional images not observable to the naked eye. She invited her therefore to join the party. At that time they were using old-fashioned polaroid cameras which presented the photographer with a little packet holding both the print and the negative. The packet was warmed in the hand for a few moments and then the print was peeled away from the negative, taking great care, for the latter was surrounded by a gummy, corrosive substance that could burn the skin. On the way out to the house they bought new polaroid film and loaded the camera outside the house.

As they drove up, they parked facing the garage or car port for the first time and realized that each corner post of the building formed a perfect gibbet. As they went in the house, now partially denuded of its furniture, Jean felt as if it were laughing at them, as much as to say, 'Hey, we won!'

Inside the house, they told John what they intended to do and then they went outside. Carol took the first picture of the front of the house, and the picture was perfect. She walked round the house and took another picture, of the outside of the dining-room in the centre of the house, and while each side of the house appeared perfectly, the dining-room area was nothing more than a panel of white light. Thinking something was wrong with the film, Carol turned and took a shot of a tree, which came out perfectly. Then she moved a little and took another shot of the house, with the dining-room on the right of the frame, and again that part of the house was obliterated by white light. Carol took a picture of the pool, the solar and the back of the house, and all the pictures turned out perfectly. But it was impossible to take a photograph of the dining-room, which was built directly above the outcrop of rock. They went to two drugstores and bought more film, so that each film was from a different place, but no matter how hard Carol tried, she could not photograph the dining-room.

As they drove away, knowing that this was the last time they would visit the place, Carol noticed that there was only one exposure left in the camera. John and Margaret were standing in front of the house waving goodbye, and Carol stuck the camera out of the car window and pressed the button.

They drove away with a certain sense of relief. It had been interesting, very interesting, but the house was still haunted and there was nothing now that they could do about it.

Carol stripped the print away from the negative and found that the final picture she had taken was a complete mess. It was underdeveloped and, 'It looked,' says Jean, 'like a dismal forest.' The people's heads seemed to be disconnected from their bodies and twisted at an odd angle. The negative, with its corrosive material, was placed carefully on the dashboard.

Two nights later Jean had friends over, and when the discussion turned on photographs, someone said that the negative was still on the dashboard of the car. Jean's husband went out and brought it in. He looked at it and asked, 'Who is the old man in the photograph?' Jean explained that there was no old man in the photograph and that, in any case, this was not a photograph but a negative. Then the negative was passed carefully from hand to hand, and in the very middle of it everyone saw the face of an old man who reminded them of Sir Matthew Begbie, though it was unlike the other photographs of him that they had seen, for in those he had dark hair and in this his hair was white and he had a white curly beard. Jean went to the library the following morning and looked out the last-taken photograph of Sir Matthew; it showed him with white hair and a white curly beard, looking exactly as he appeared in the negative taken in 1978, so many years after his death.

Most hauntings can be explained, once the necessary research has been done, and once an exorcism has been performed, the ghostly manifestations cease. The house on the hill, however, defeated the exorcists. It is still standing there, and though it occupied a large area, that land has not been subdivided and built upon, as has the other land around. The house now looks decrepit; it has lost all its old elegance; and the atmosphere on entering the driveway is more than unpleasant.

What explanation is there? One suggestion is that a vortex may have been created by the confluence of crossing the ley lines, those lines of electro-magnetic force on the earth's surface that, in combination, create the earth's own magnetic field. These lines are not only receptive to ghosts but are productive of all kinds of psychic and spiritual phenomena. Burial mounds, churches, holy wells, even schools and hospitals can often be joined together by a straight line on the map, and ley lines in Britain have been found to link many of the key cathedrals. When ley lines come together or cross, their effect is increased to such an extent that a vortex capable of drawing into it a great many of the surrounding spiritual energy forms may be created.

Radio-activity may also be a reason for the vortex in the house on the hill, for when granite ages and decays, it becomes radio-active, and the rock in the basement may therefore be responsible for many of the phenomena. Moreover, a rock of this kind would attract anyone wandering alone in meditation and without a fixed purpose, as Sir Matthew Baillie Begbie wandered. After his retirement he grew very ill indeed of a cancer from which he eventually died, and as an old man, in pain and contemplating his own death, he may well have left a memory imprint upon the place. This would account for the capital M upon the mirror. He had not been a vicious judge; indeed, he had been a devout Christian and a just and sensible man; consequently in surveying his past, as he must have on those lonely wanderings as he sat in solitude upon that rock, he is likely to have brought to mind those executions he had ordered and attended, and this might account for the number of times images of hanging, of twisted necks or of painful backs occurred. It might even account for the push in the back that several people felt at the top of the basement stairs and that Priscilla felt in the entrance to the room with the rock.

All this is only supposition. Nothing can be proved, but if the rock is indeed radio-active and forms a vortex of energy, it is understandable that the effects of any exorcism would not be permanent. The house on the hill remains a centre of pain and depression, a gathering-place for unhappiness.

2

Murder!

Many of the most famous ghosts that have been placed on record are spectres of people who have been murdered or executed, or who have died unexpectedly. It seems that when somebody meets death without forewarning the spirit is confused, does not believe, indeed, that death has occurred and continues to attempt life on the physical plane, distressed and crying for attention from the living. A sudden and violent death can also cause a surge of astonishment and terror, and these emotions may leave an imprint on the place where the death occurred, whether or not the spirit of the dead person continues to haunt the earthly plane. Some murdered or executed people haunt not merely the place of their deaths but the places to which they were attached during their earthly existence; this explains the numerous places that have been haunted by Mary, Queen of Scots, and Anne Boleyn and suggests a reason why Dick Turpin, the highwayman, does not haunt the place where he was hanged but some of the roads along which he travelled.

Jean's first encounter with a ghost was caused by a sudden death which may or may not have been murder. She encountered it when she was a small child, and it puzzled rather than alarmed her. She could not understand why none of the adults around her could see it, and was obliged to dismiss the phenomenon as just one of those things to which adults chose to pay no attention, or to which they were blind because of their age.

It all took place in the early thirties, when hopeful athletes had begun to prepare themselves for the summer Olympics of 1936, which were to be held in Berlin. Jean was staying in Muskoka at a summer hotel owned by her grandfather. The place delighted her.

'It was only accessible by boat,' she says, 'and one of the wonderful extras was a lovely natural spring whose water was always cold, and the touch of the metal dipper hung by a chain on a nearby tree always caused a tiny pang of pain when it touched your teeth. You could sit and watch that spring for hours; it was just one wonderful bubble which would rise and burst, and then there would be a moment of silence and stillness before another bubble slowly rose and burst in its turn.

'I was not old enough to go to school, and so I was treated like an infant by the grown-ups. I had only a vague impression of events outside our retreat, and so knew nothing about the Olympics that were about to take place until, one day, two gorgeous young people arrived to stay at the hotel. He was dark, handsome, solidly built and even a little chunky; she was small and slim, with short blonde hair parted on one side, straight except for a few rigid waves and a froth of curls at the bottom. We were told that they were swimmers about to take part in the Olympics and that they were on their honeymoon, – but I cannot of course vouch for the accuracy of either of these statements. They chatted with us all for a little while and then they went off together. They were training themselves by swimming in the lakes and rivers round about, and were all prepared to go in the water. The man was wearing a black bathing-suit with long legs and broad shoulder straps; his wife's one-piece suit also had long legs, and the upper half was striped red, white and yellow.

'A little way away from the hotel there were rapids that they had already handled with ease, and also a narrow canyon of water with a small island in the centre that led to a very strong whirlpool with a powerful undertow. They were warned about this by the adults, but the young man must have thought little of the warning, for he laughed as they walked away from us.

'It was about half an hour later that he came stumbling back up the path alone, stopping several times to be sick. He gasped out that his wife had been caught in the whirlpool and had gone down and he had been unable to find her. I thought he was crazy, because I could see her standing behind him, weeping. She was wet, as if she had just been pulled out of the water, and doubled over as if in pain, crying, 'How could you? How could you?' Everyone went running off to launch boats and get swimsuits, and I thought it was just another case of adults behaving in a stupid way. After all, there she was, behind him, and all that day she followed him, tears running down her cheeks. As he asked for help and went off with the search party and later returned to have something to eat, she was always there, just a few feet behind him.

'The body was never recovered, and later a small cement cross was placed on the island in the middle of the canyon. All that summer, until I went to school in the fall, I would see her. I would stand on the highest point of the many pathways around the hotel and look down over the island and see her there, bent over in pain as if she had been hit in the stomach. She was calling, "Why did he do it? I loved him!" Somehow, although she was quite a distance away, I could always hear the words. Later that year, after my first experience of school, I came back to the hotel, but she was gone.

'Two weeks after the drowning my mother came home and went upstairs to change into a bathing-suit. When she emerged from the house, everyone gasped, for she was wearing a new suit identical to that of the drowned woman. She was forbidden to wear it and had to be satisfied with the previous year's model.

'Years later, my grandmother, when someone was talking of the drowning, said, "It was a double tragedy. The child was pregnant." Someone asked her how she knew. "A woman would know," she said.'

It is not, of course, clear whether or not the husband had intended to drown his wife. It may have been a terrible accident, for which she blamed him. It seems, however, that she did not continue to haunt the place where she had died in order to warn others of the danger of the whirlpool, as has happened in a number of other instances of drowning. It would be leaping to an irresponsible conclusion to think that the ghost's cry of 'How could you?' pointed to a deliberate murder. It is more probable that it was a terrible accident for which she blamed him in her confusion.

Ghosts do, indeed, attempt to influence the living, and sometimes appear to people who are in real danger, or in a situation the dead person considers dangerous because of his or her own experience. This is the case with Victoria's most famous ghost, who haunts the Oak Bay Golf Course. It is the ghost of Doris Gravlin, whose strangled body was discovered buried there in a sand-trap. Suspicion immediately fell upon her husband, Victor, for theirs had been a turbulent marriage. Indeed, they had lived apart more often than not, he more or less regularly in a house on Oak Bay Avenue, and she at a variety of addresses, for she was a nurse and was sometimes required to live in the homes of her patients.

It was their custom of Sunday afternoons to walk across the golf course to enjoy tea at the Oak Bay Beach Hotel, and sometimes they would also take this walk of an evening. Victor had been seen walking on the golf course with Doris on the Sunday evening immediately before the body was discovered. The gossip of the time stated that she had been carrying a large sum of money in her purse and that Victor had strangled her and spent the money on rum. The story was hardly covered by the local paper, perhaps because Victor worked for it as a reporter, and his uncle had an executive position with it. Victor was never arrested, for the investigation had only just got under way when he drowned himself. Doris's ghost has been appearing on the Oak Bay Golf Course ever since, usually at the end of March, though sometimes a little earlier. The label 'April Ghost' which has been in use ever since the hauntings began is therefore not wholly accurate, but Doris does appear in April also.

The hauntings began in 1936, and since that year Doris's spectre has appeared with some regularity in two different areas and at two different times. Between 4.30 and 5 p.m. she has been seen walking across the golf course, looking entirely normal, though slightly old-fashioned. It is only when she has passed by that the watcher feels anything unusual and experiences a kind of dread as Doris turns and looks back over her shoulder. Later, between 9.30 and 10 in the evening she appears on the golf course close to the water. She stands with her arms outstretched, wearing a long white dress. She rushes towards you, then suddenly she shrinks into a small pool of light and disappears. In this particular guise she appears only to courting or engaged couples, and never to married persons, who perceive a different phenomenon.

One day when Jean was taking part in a radio talk show and discussing the April Ghost, she received a phone call from a Texan tourist. On the previous night he and a male friend had been driving along Beach Drive towards the Oak Bay Beach Hotel. They came to an intersection and stopped, and saw a young woman in a long white dress cross in front of them, going towards the sea. They thought nothing of it, but when a few blocks later they stopped at a second intersection and again saw a young woman wearing a long white dress crossing in front of them and making her way towards the sea, they each felt a growing tension, though they said nothing to each other. Three blocks farther on a young woman wearing a long white fluffy dress was standing at the intersection observing them, and the passenger said, in terror, 'For God's sake, don't stop!' They did not stop, nor did they talk about what they had seen or the unreasoning terror that had overcome them, until they heard Jean discussing the April Ghost on the radio. Then they realized that they had encountered Doris.

Another sighting took place on 12 March 1972. Patrick Dunae and Fiona Gow were walking on the golf course at 9.45 p.m. They both wrote down what they had experienced. Fiona Gow wrote:

> We turned onto the golf course at approximately 9.45 and walked in a straight line towards the sea. Discovering that the land closest to the sea was no better than marsh, we turned and walked up the course parallel to Beach Drive. On our right side rocks and bushes obscured all view of the

sea. As we walked we were both struck by the extreme stillness of the night and by the relative mildness of the air. Having gained the top of the slight ascent which forms a greater part of the golf course, and at the same time passed the last clump of trees, I turned and saw a white squarish shape, shining between myself and the sea. The shape appeared to be at quite a distance, its most extraordinary characteristic being a strange luminosity similar to that of a very brightly shining white light. In shape the object was quite large, being slightly more tall than broad and coming to a point at the top. During the time which it took us to reach the road the apparition appeared to remain in the same place. I would judge that all these events took place about 10.

Fiona Gow was at that time a mature University of Victoria student, as was her companion, Patrick Dunae. His version of the experience agrees with that of his friend:

At approximately 9.45 p.m. on March 12th Fiona Gow and I were walking north-east from Newport Avenue along the Victoria Golf Course – on the side closest to the water. It was a very dark, but warm, night. The mist seemed to soften everything and we had commented on the silence. As we were about 200 yards along our way (and just nearing a slight rise past the sand traps) Fiona started and turned towards me. I looked behind her and saw a white, softly luminous object – roughly rectangular in shape. I too was startled since it seemed suddenly to have 'appeared' about 100 yards to our right (near the water). But as it was surrounded by a clump of trees I presumed that it had just come into view as we began to climb the rise. I dismissed it as a green-keeper's house but, as Fiona was still frightened, we turned left to make for the road. I looked over my shoulder, a number of times as we were heading for the road and the 'shape' was still visible where we had first seen it. Jokingly I admitted that it did seem to have an 'ethereal' presence, but we continued towards the road, stepped over the wire fence, and returned south-west on Beach Drive.

After hearing that there was supposed to be an 'April Ghost', we returned the next day to see if there was in fact

> a house visible from where we had seen the object. We were unable to see any such house after re-walking our course.

In talking to the press, both friends elaborated a little on their experience. Fiona described the apparition as 'almost Christmas-tree shaped' and was reported as feeling that it was the stereotype of a 'woman in a sheet'. Patrick described it as 'white, soft, luminous and regular'.

Shortly after Patrick Dunae and Fiona Gow had their experience, Jean and her friends decided that the phenomenon should be investigated a little further. Therefore at the beginning of April they formed a committee to organize regular surveillance. They asked people to go out, two by two, in the evening during the week beginning 17 April and see what was happening. They asked them to take photographs of various parts of the golf course, hoping that they might, by chance, pick up an extra figure or shadow or patch of light on the photographs. Everybody promised to go, but nobody went.

Therefore one night Jean, Cece, Tara and Betty decided that, as the time of the haunting was coming to an end, they should themselves visit the scene. It was a clear, cool evening after a warm, dry day. The time was about 9.15 and the temperature was 51° Fahrenheit. There was no wind, no cloud, no moon. They parked the car beside the road, and immediately three of the group saw a tall, thin white figure crossing the golf course in a south-easterly direction. Although it moved very quickly, it appeared to be gliding rather than walking, for the movement was smooth and not in the slightest jerky. In a moment it was gone, and they could not be absolutely certain whether they had seen a spectre or a play of shadows. It had not gone behind a hill or a tree, however; it had simply vanished; the light had gone out. They stayed around for about an hour and then went home, having no further plan in mind. They had only wished to feel the place out.

Three days later, on another warm clear evening with a few clouds in the sky but no moon, they ventured out once more. It was ten o'clock when they reached the golf course, and the thermometer stood at 48° Fahrenheit. One of their purposes was to watch the passing cars on the road to see if their lights could possibly cause the effect of this white figure crossing the hill. As they got out of the car, the wind began suddenly to whistle around them. It was impossible to tell from what direction it was blowing; it seemed to be coming from everywhere at once, and their hair and clothing were blown in all directions at the same time. Cece, who had recently sat through a number of quite frightening seances and had remained absolutely calm and collected, suddenly became very upset and nervous, and even slightly hysterical. She screamed several times at dark shadows. They all joined hands and attempted to create energy but could not do so. At least forty cars drove by on the road, and the lights of three of them did appear to reveal a running figure. However, they could not work out why only three of the forty sets of headlights had caused this phenomenon.

The wind grew even wilder and as they walked back to the car someone took Jean's hand and they walked along together for a few feet. Jean says, 'I remember thinking, "Poor thing, she really must be frightened; her hand is so cold." Then looking ahead I realized that the whole group was walking ahead of me, and the hand seemed to fade away. As we got to the car looking over the golf course, Betty said, 'Put your hand in mine" and as I took her hand a cold wind was blowing down the sleeve of her coat and creating an eddy in her hand.'

They decided that they had had enough and went back to Jean's house, which was only six blocks away, and as they stepped out of the car they realized that it was a lovely warm evening with not a breath of wind.

The ghost of Doris has been seen and felt by a great many people over the years. Indeed, in 1980 a group of teenagers, friends of my daughters, descended upon our home in some alarm because they had seen her, and I had to explain to them that there was nothing to be scared about. This was only a little disingenuous, for it does seem that those courting or engaged couples who see her in her long white dress, her arms outstretched, and watch her shrink away into a little pool of light before vanishing entirely, never do get married. Doris, understandably, appears to be opposed to matrimony.

Some ghosts do, indeed, appear to have strong views on various subjects, and especially on those connected with their own difficulties or their sudden deaths. In one particular case, however, it was not the murdered ones who caused the greatest disturbance but their murderer, and he was still alive and sent to prison in 1977.

'It was,' Jean says, 'my first encounter with a convicted murderer.' She had been called in to investigate a house troubled by disturbances. The house was large, three-storeyed and in a style that might be called 'heritage'. There were built-in china cabinets, with bevelled glass in the doors and also in some of the windows. The downstairs rooms comprised home for Elizabeth and her two young children, 10-year-old Beth and 3-year-old George, who had been named after his father, the murderer, who was now in prison. The stairs to the basement were steep, and the basement itself was very cold and damp. On the second floor there was a large sitting-room, a bedroom and a bathroom, forming almost a separate apartment, though there was no kitchen. The rooms appeared to be occupied by a man, but Elizabeth did not say who was living there and was reluctant to let Jean go upstairs. Jean did not feel that the second floor was relevant to the happenings downstairs, and so was not unduly frustrated, but the upstairs apartment did feel suspicious, as if something underhand was occurring in the rooms.

The killing for which Elizabeth's husband had been convicted was not his first. Twelve years earlier he had killed a man with his bare hands, and the judge at his trial, taking into consideration that he was a new immigrant and a refugee from the Hungarian revolution of 1956, had merely fined him $50. 'The Red Devil', as the Hungarian community called him, thereafter often maintained that $50 was the price of a human life in Canada and that, if he was enraged enough, he was quite ready to pay for the privilege of despatching anybody who got in his way.

Unfortunately he felt that two young people, Sandy and Jill, were in his way; they had, it appears, displeased him over some drug deal, and though they had both been so close to his family and friendly with his children as almost to be family themselves, he killed them. Their bodies were found, immediately after their deaths, in a house on Fort Street. The Red Devil was arrested, tried, found guilty and sent to prison.

The Red Devil had been in prison for two years when Jean was called in to investigate the goings-on in the house. The children appeared to be the focal point of the various happenings. Ten-year-old Beth was having some success as a child model; her bedroom was filled with glossy photographs of her work, some of them a little sleazy, a little too sexy, though they fell far short of pornography.

Three-year-old George was also modelling. He was an unusual child, so well developed that he looked like an eight-year-old. His conversation was quite the equal of his sister's. His unusual qualities had revealed themselves early. When only three days old, he had somehow or other levitated a dummy from the dresser to his crib. Aged six months he had broken a metal music box with his bare hands and had laughed at the dismay on his mother's face. At eighteen months he was walking, talking, telling stories with plots, characters and moral endings.

Nevertheless, Elizabeth was not perturbed, for her husband was now in prison and she was enjoying a new life with her children. The Red Devil had not been a good husband to her; not long after they had moved into the house he had begun beating her, and she had been terrified of him. Indeed he had been feared by all who knew him, and his use of drugs and alcohol had made him even more unstable. Elizabeth had known about the murder of Sandy and Jill for three months before he had been arrested and charged, and had kept silent out of sheer terror. It was, she felt, a blessing that he was gone.

Her peace of mind, however, was not to last. Odd happenings

occurred. George had fallen down a steep ten-foot flight of stairs, and his older sister claimed that two giant hands had caught him and placed him safely on the floor, absolutely uninjured. He sat there laughing as his mother looked on in horror.

Both Beth and George told her they had been seeing Jill and Sandy, the two murdered young people, in the house. Beth added that they had both talked to Jill in their bedroom a few hours before the bodies were discovered. Her father, she said, had threatened her when he heard of this and told her to shut up about it and never mention Jill again. Now, however, Elizabeth told Jean, Jill had returned and was not only talking to Beth but also hitting her in the chest. Beth frequently cried out in her bed at night because Jill was being 'so mean'.

Little George had also been affected. He had become very aggressive and swore uncontrollably, just like his father. Elizabeth also had been troubled. She maintained that she felt 'presences' and that her legs were always cold. In her bedroom she often became almost overcome with fear, and in the early evening she sensed a man's presence in the room over by the bay window and was convinced that it was the male murder victim, Sandy, seeking revenge. In the early evening the presence was also observed several times in the master bedroom; the air seemed to become almost thick, as if a solid shadow were standing in the window.

Jean tried to make contact with this 'presence' but received no response. She felt that his particular presence was the heart of the matter, however, and that if it could be removed the visits of Jill and Sandy would also cease. In order to get a clearer view of the situation, she talked to a friend in the penal service who was working in the prison where the Red Devil was confined. He told her that early every evening George would sit in his cell facing the wall and remain there, absolutely still, for as long as two hours. The prison guards said, 'It's as if he isn't even there. He doesn't respond to either noise or conversation.' One guard said, 'Man, it's as if he's *gone*!'

The Red Devil had, indeed, 'gone'; he had gone back to his

home to keep an eye on what was happening, to save little George from disaster and teach him to swear, and to torment and frighten his mother.

Jean endeavoured to explain the situation to Elizabeth but was never quite sure that Elizabeth understood what she was being told. In order to weaken the link between the Red Devil and his sometime home, she asked Elizabeth to take down a large oil painting of her husband which hung in the living-room. Elizabeth refused, saying that it was very important for the children to remember what their father was like. Jean therefore took another tack. As the family was Catholic, she persuaded and helped Elizabeth to set up a small altar in the bay window where the presence had most usually appeared, making use of as many sacred objects as she could find. She asked her also to place holy water, obtained from her priest, upon the altar. Once this was done, the presence never returned.

When the Red Devil was about to be released from prison, Elizabeth left Victoria and attempted to start a modelling school for children. Later she sold spells and potions by mail, and Jean realized that she had been less interested in discovering the truth about the disturbances than in getting some relief from them at the same time as some confirmation of the dramatic nature of her experiences and her psychic abilities. She was now calling herself 'Erica the Witch'.

Elizabeth's fascination with the occult and her enjoyment of the dramatic had, actually, been revealed earlier, when she had told of little George, who, one must remember, was not yet four years old, telling stories of two separate past lives that he had experienced. Jean had listened to a tape recording of these stories but had noticed that Elizabeth was prompting her son a good deal of the time. Therefore she took both children out to supper, where they could speak without their mother's interference or assistance. Over the meal both Beth and George admitted that their tales of past lives had been cobbled together from television programmes they had seen, and that George had simply been trying to frighten his mother. The children were very competitive and precocious, eager to cap each other's stories and capture Jean's interest. They did, however, insist that the story of Jill's ghost was entirely true and that the tale of the giant hand was true also. George said, indeed, with firm conviction, that it was Daddy, who had promised always to take care of him. And in this George was probably entirely correct.

Whether a murderer's victim or a murderer, whether dead or alive, it seems that the human creature, when possessed by a passionate need to communicate, can produce presences, apparitions and physical phenomena that disturb the lives of others.

3

Look Out for the Vampire

The first time Jean and I worked together involved a ghost that I can only say had vampire tendencies; it drained away the vitality of the householder until she had to be hospitalized, and it was a very possessive ghost indeed.

Jean says:

'The house on St David Street was very important to both Robin and me for very different reasons. It was a very beautiful house on a street in Oak Bay, and, more importantly, it was Sandra's house.

'I first met Sandra when she phoned and asked for an interview on witchcraft which was an assignment for a course she was taking at the University of Victoria. She arrived late one afternoon, a beauty with dark hair, a Mickey Mouse T-shirt and a charming little-girl voice that I had heard only in Ontario at fine upper-class schools like Loretta Abbey or at tea dances at the Granite Club. She was immediately a friend. We could talk and understand each other without a myriad explanations. Several hours over herbal tea and cookies cemented a friendship that has grown over the years. She is one of those very special people that you can meet after years apart and continue right where you left off, with no guilty feelings and no reminders of "You never phoned me." Later we found out that we had friends in common, and I discovered, to my surprise, that she was a single mother of three living in a wonderful house in Oak Bay that she had purchased almost by magic.'

When Jean met Sandra, I had been a friend of hers (Sandra's) for some time. I encountered her first when she and her then husband were living at 1255 Victoria Avenue and offering the house for sale, although she already knew my wife, Sylvia, from their work together on the Women's Committee of the Art Gallery. We bought the house, which was in wonderful condition and beautifully decorated by Sandra's own hands. Later Sandra took part in a movie that I co-wrote and co-directed, and we visited her both at her new home before she moved to St David Street, and also at the St David Street house, which I myself had visited in 1962 and which she redecorated and renewed until it was something of a showplace.

Sandra completed her assignment with Jean and continued studying at the university, but the next few years were difficult for her. Motherhood, work and study seemed to have sapped her strength, and finally the doctor diagnosed very low blood pressure. He said she was exhibiting all the signs of extreme old age. She was put into hospital, but one night's stay there caused all her symptoms mysteriously to disappear, and soon a pattern began to emerge.

This pattern of low blood pressure, a day or two in the hospital and then total recovery was so remarkable that Jean felt the house itself must be in some way responsible. I agreed with her, and Sylvia, my wife, was emphatic. 'Robin, you must DO something,' she said. I, of course, did not know quite what to do, but I shared her sense of urgency. I also shared her suspicions of the house. When we arrived in Victoria together in 1963, the house had been available for rent, and as the owners, whom I had visited the previous year when I spent a summer in Victoria, were friends, they offered it to us. Sylvia went round the house with me but rejected it. She said it smelt of cat and was dirty. It was an odd criticism, for we have always been cat-lovers and quite impervious to feline odours, and the house was not dirty at all. I registered the clear fact that Sylvia had 'taken against' the house, and we did not move in. Our friends who wanted to rent out the house were then at a difficult point in their marriage, and they divorced shortly afterwards.

Jean began to go into the history of the house with her usual thoroughness. She reported that one owner of the house had had a brain tumour that disappeared when she left the house to live in an apartment. One person had bought the house and never moved in. One person had committed suicide and another had died from a drug overdose. The house had, indeed, a long history of illness and disaster.

Sylvia was obviously correct. Something had to be done.

By this time I had met Jean. Indeed, it was Sandra who brought us together in her living-room at the house in St David Street. Jean and I liked each other immediately, though I, for one, was at first a little cautious, for one of Sandra's most engaging qualities is her enthusiasm for anything novel, and another is her tendency to overpraise her friends. However, in this instance, the two people she introduced managed to discard the weight of Sandra's praise of each to the other, and to discount her bubbling enthusiasm, and in a very short time indeed we were talking like the fast friends we became.

It was therefore quite natural when something had to be done for Jean and me to visit Sandra and look the house over together. This may sound as if we were a pair of psychic sponges, eager to suck up into ourselves whatever spookiness we could find. This is not really how it works. For the greater part of the time one does not 'switch on' one's receiving apparatus; one simply observes and talks and uses one's commonsense. It is only when it is necessary to become hypersensitive that one 'switches on'. On this occasion I myself did feel it necessary to switch on, however.

Jean says: 'I watched Robin to find out his way of working, and realized that he "breathes" a house. Using his left hand and gently balancing his energy into areas of the room, following subtle changes in energy, he wanders to disturbed spots and breathes in shallowly, tasting and feeling the atmosphere. Leaving him, I walked through the house charting high energy points, and later we met in the dining-room to compare notes.'

A spot on the stairs, one in the upper hallway, the whole dining-room, the servants' staircase and a window in the kitchen were uncomfortable for both of us. In the kitchen between the stove and the sink there also was a patch of cold. Walking through it was like walking through an invisible refrigerator.

After we had done our own exploring, Sandra told us of her experiences in the house. The kitchen often made her nervous and depressed. On one occasion she had felt herself to be imprisoned there and unable to go upstairs to her children because of some force on the stairs. She had said, out loud, 'You can't come between me and my children!' When Sandra told us of these words, Jean says, 'I heard an echo of a man's voice saying the same thing, and I put that down in my notebook. I felt it was important, and that the sentence she spoke was an echo of something that had happened in the past.'

Sandra found the basement, especially in the vicinity of the furnace, very unpleasant, and the lights in the upper floor of the house would sometimes flicker or go on and off for no reason. Although she was always deeply interested in interior decoration and had, indeed, made our Victoria Avenue house into a most graceful and beautiful place when she owned it, she was more than normally troubled by the dining-room in the St David Street House. I remember her saying, intensely, that it did not 'feel right' and asking my advice. She never seemed to feel wholly comfortable there. It was in the dining-room that her son Shawn, who was the most affected by psychic phenomena of all the children, had an alarming experience. Sitting at table, he became involved in an argument with his mother and, growing angry, stood up and threw his napkin down on the table; it burst into flames.

I suggested, as an interim procedure, that Sandra, who loved paintings, should hang a painting or print containing the eye symbol in the room. The eye symbol is an ancient one that in many cultures, from Egyptian to Pacific Native, is regarded as guarding, watching out for danger and thus bringing good fortune.

Jean continued research on the background of the house. She discovered that some time in the early 1900s one of Victoria's leading citizens, a widower with grown-up children, had travelled to Barkerville, where he met and was enthralled by

Mae, an exciting, somewhat tawdry dance-hall girl. He wooed and won and wed her and brought her back to the house on St David Street. The honeymoon magic soon disappeared as his children and Victorian society in general failed to accept her. Their life together was short. He died, leaving her alone in the house. Several years later a handsome young 'nephew' moved in. A marriage was announced but within a few months Mae found herself alone again, for the bridegroom had disappeared. Mae went on living in the house on her own, becoming steadily more and more eccentric. She developed a fear of stoves, which led to her cooking meat in a toaster-like arrangement in the furnace. This odd little fact became extremely significant as our researches into the ghost continued.

During this time of investigation Sandra's situation did not improve. One day she invited Jean and me and some other friends for lunch. She placed a very generous meal on the dining-room table, then turned and walked back into the kitchen and said, 'Why did I invite all these people? I don't have enough food. They won't enjoy it here!' Then she returned to the table and said, with an air of surprise, 'There's plenty of food; it looks great!' As she went back into the kitchen and again became disturbed by doubts, Jean and I looked at each other and realized that when she stood beside the stove she became irrational and eccentric, adding to the symptoms of extreme old age mentioned by the doctor. We knew that Mae was overshadowing and possessing Sandra.

The distinction between a haunting and a possession is not always easy to make. It is largely a question of degree. If the ghost merely disturbs a person, it is not a case of possession, but if that disturbance leads to a character change or a change in the victim's health, the term 'possession' becomes appropriate. When a ghost 'takes over' a person, however briefly, one must think of possession as being at least an element in the situation, though the possession may be very brief and only in certain places or at certain times.

Through Sandra, Mae had the house, the social position, important friends, three beautiful children, indeed everything that she had been denied when she lived on St David Street herself. An exorcism was now a necessity.

Before the exorcism could be planned, we had to arrange for the children to be lodged elsewhere; it is not wise to perform an exorcism when young children are present, for they may be not only puzzled and frightened but also physically affected by the proceedings. It is important in an exorcism for all parties not only to know what is going on but to concentrate their minds and energies in a fashion quite impossible to the very young. The children therefore were driven over to my own house, where Sylvia was to look after them until the exorcism was over and the house cleansed.

Exorcisms all follow the same basic pattern, and we have given details of a complete exorcism ceremony in an appendix, so do not need to give a step-by-step account of it here. The house was sealed from the inside with incense, and on the table by the front door were set three candlesticks with three candles, the middle one being mauve and the flanking ones white; oil, bread, salt, wine, water and flowers were also placed on the table. The group gathered together for the ceremony consisted of Jean, myself, Sandra, Jean's friend and colleague Cece, and Sandra's close friend Joyce.

We began the ceremony at 9 p.m., and as soon as the ghost had been commanded to appear before us, the flame of the central candle of the three flickered. I noticed particularly that the flames of the two neighbouring candles did not stir at all. It was my first exorcism, and I was fascinated. Jean told us that clearly we had only to deal with one ghost, otherwise the two other candles would have flickered also.

I was, I must admit, wondering if I was not being a little credulous, but as soon as the ceremony began, my faint doubt disappeared, for, as Jean says, 'Mae became so real a person during the ceremony that we all became emotionally involved. This was dangerous. We felt her pain and were dangerously sympathetic to her.' It is, of course, unwise to feel too sympathetic towards a ghost in these circumstances; it is too much like acceptance. One must somehow preserve a proper distance.

Still, as Jean says, 'To save Sandra it was necessary to send Mae away. We tried to reason with Mae. She wanted so much to stay. We finally asked Sandra to expel her. The command had to come from her, and she had to be unsympathetic and strong and very very resolute. Finally, Sandra heard her say, with a sigh, "I must say goodbye to this dear old house." I replied, "You may remain until the mauve candle goes out. Then you must leave, never to return." The candle was now less than half an inch long, and the time was eleven o'clock.

'We went into the dining-room to have refreshments, and to talk among ourselves. Every few minutes someone would check the candle. It slowly consumed itself until finally there was only melted wax and a blue flame the size of the head of a wooden match.'

I was fascinated by this flame, and at one point I stood looking staring at it for several minutes. There was no vestige of wick left; there was nothing to feed the flame; it was, indeed, a flame subsisting entirely on its own energy. Mae was clearly most reluctant to leave. 'We're paying her too much attention,' I said, 'Let's ignore her.' So we turned our backs and went back to the dining-room from the front hall where the candle was burning. At 2 p.m. Sandra summoned up all her positive thinking and phoned Sylvia to say that we would be leaving in a few minutes, because the candle would soon be going out. Positive thinking was not, however, enough. The flame went on burning and continued to burn as we drank more coffee and washed the dishes. Two-thirty, three and 3.30 came and went. At ten minutes past four the phone rang and Sylvia's voice said, 'Sandra, the children …'. At that moment three heavy knocks sounded on the front door, and as Jean passed the table, a small strain of grey smoke wafted upwards as the flame finally went out. There was no one at the door.

When a house has been emptied of an energy that has occupied it for many years, a kind of vacuum is created. The house is, indeed, vulnerable. It is open to anything to fill the void that has been created. Therefore one must fill the emptiness with blessings. Each one of us picked up something from the table and went to a place we felt to be an important part of the house, indeed essential to its health and the health of the inhabitants. Joyce took the bread and went into the kitchen and blessed the area around the stove. Cece picked up the flowers and put them in the living-room, for she was so awed by the beauty of the house that she felt this beauty to be central to its character. I went upstairs with a glass of wine in my hand and delivered what Jean has told me since was a joyful but somewhat bawdy blessing on the master bedroom. I have no recollection of what I said. The words were wholly spontaneous. I responded simply and intuitively to the moment.

Jean warned Sandra that, although the house had now been blessed and the vacuum filled, there might be disturbances of a poltergeist-like kind during the following twenty-four hours, and, indeed, when the children, roused by Sylvia from the beds and couches where she had been obliged to place them when they could no longer stay awake, still half asleep and rubbing their eyes, returned, the lights upstairs flickered off and on several times.

Jean instructed Sandra on the next necessary step. In the morning she had to dig a hole in the garden, in a place that was unlikely to be disturbed. Every scrap of wax scraped out of the candlesticks, the loaf of bread and the flowers had to be placed in the hole and covered with earth, and then the salt, water and wine poured upon the place.

Sandra slept late, and the next day it was almost one o'clock before she got around to this concluding part of the ceremony. Burying a loaf of bread and some dead flowers in a backyard in Oak Bay in front of all the neighbours, and then pouring salt, water and wine over it all, struck Sandra as being inclined to cause comment but nevertheless, feeling somewhat absurd and giggling at herself, she performed the task.

The exorcism proved to have been successful. Not long after it had been performed, Sandra, at a party, met the couple from whom she had bought the house. They had lived in it for only a short time, having bought it sight-unseen through an agent. They had done this because the husband, then living in Britain, had been offered a post in Victoria, and he did not wish to spend the time and money involved in coming out ahead of time to hunt for a house in which to live. The man's wife told Sandra that she wished to apologize to her for selling the house without admitting that it was haunted, but she had been afraid that they would never sell the house at all if they made that confession.

A further patch of the house's history came to light a little later, when Sylvia was talking to the friend who had offered it to us for rent when we first came to Victoria in 1963. She told Sylvia that she was sure the house had affected her then husband adversely, for she often woke in the night and looked at him and was sure he had died, for he looked so pale and cadaverous.

The unpleasantness had now, however, vanished. Sandra was happy in the house. She raised her children successfully, completed her education, started a successful career, married again and finally found a new home. The house on St David Street was put on the market and was admired by many people, but for a year and a half nobody offered to buy it. Jean and I suggested that she make it a little less attractive, for the rooms were all so elegantly decorated and furnished, and Sandra had so many splendid pictures and *objets d'art*, that we felt prospective purchasers might be put off by feeling that this was a house they had to live up to. It didn't help.

I tried a spell to help the process along, but it was not successful.

'Finally,' says Jean, 'We decided that Sandra had made the house so definitely hers that no one else could visualize it as being theirs. One evening Joyce, Cece, Sandra, Robin and I met in the living-room and, after drinking a glass of white wine, we began another ceremony. We started at the top of the house and worked our way down. Cece had a handful of wooden skewers from Chinatown; they were sharp at one end and blunt at the other. In each room Sandra was handed a skewer and asked to remember important things that had happened there. If they were painful, she was to press the sharp end against her thumb, and if they were pleasant, the blunt one. When she had remembered the event in detail, she was to break the skewer, and thus release herself from bondage to that memory.

'If Sandra had asked us for help when she first put the house on the market, we would have suggested a very simple ceremony with candles and released the house from its bondage to her at that time. The ritual is to burn one black and one white candle for two hours, saying nothing, but just leaving them to burn in a safe place. This burns out the positive and negative energies in the house. After the black and white candles have burned out, one should place an orange candle in the living-room and one in the bedroom, and say as they are lit, "I release all personal influences within this house, in order that it may be sold in joy and light to a new owner".'

'Since Sandra had not done this, before we began the ceremony with the skewers we lit two orange candles and let them burn during the whole ceremony. As we lit them she said, "In the name of light may this house be released from my ownership and be sold immediately to another person. I, as the present owner, have enjoyed the comfort and protection of the house, but now I wish to release it to new owners so that I may have a home that reflects my present needs".'

'As Sandra took the sticks and recalled all that had happened in the house, she sometimes told us the memory, so that we could share it, and join her in breaking the bond. Occasionally, however, she smiled and told us nothing; sometimes there were tears in her eyes. As we moved from room to room, she had so many memories that we thought we were going to run out of sticks, although we had begun with 300, but the supply lasted until it was all over. When she broke a stick, she handed it to me, and by the time we had returned to the living-room where we had begun, I had a host of them. I placed them in the living-room fireplace and burned them, saying that memories now no longer chained the house to Sandra, or Sandra to the house, and blessing the house with peace.'

After the ceremony we all had wine and cheese and home-baked bread in the dining-room. Within two days Sandra received the first offer on the house, and it was sold almost immediately.

4

The Chinese Curse

The phone-call was from a woman who said her niece was in trouble, and would Jean please help her. The address was Henry Hudson Apartments, and 308 was situated down a hall and past a heavy fire door. The troubled residents were called Donna and Bill.

Bill was a Victoria policeman and was very young, with squeaky-clean blond good looks. His family came from Ottawa. He was studying for his promotion, and the dining-room of the apartment was lined with metal shelves filled with books and games and puzzles designed to challenge the mind. He had met and married Donna in Victoria. Donna was a local girl with many relations in the area. She was rather a plain, wholesome-looking girl and seemed even more so beside her handsome husband, but over the months that followed, her charm and personality enchanted Jean and her friends, and Bill rather faded into the background.

The bedroom was clearly the heart of the house, cosy and comfortable, and though the apartment as a whole seemed to be crammed to capacity with boxes and files, it was not dirty or cluttered, only crowded.

The trouble had begun when Bill's mother had paid the couple a visit. Neither of his parents had been present at the wedding, and so she had not met Donna previously. She could stay for only a few days and so a full agenda of sightseeing was arranged. They rented a car and drove north from Victoria to show off the beauty of Vancouver Island. The trip was pleasant, and everyone seemed to be getting along just fine. At a very narrow point on the steep Malahat Drive, on the way home, Bill felt something or someone take the wheel and turn the car into the rock wall at the side of the road. He fought for control of the car and then managed to step on the brakes. Not wanting to alarm anyone and feeling a little foolish about letting his imagination get away from him, he blamed the incident on the car. Later that night, unable to sleep, he told Donna what had really happened.

The rest of the visit was pleasant and uneventful. Bill's mother had enjoyed Victoria; she seemed to like Donna and, indeed, one morning got up early and left without having breakfast in order to buy them a very special wedding present. At the end of the visit they drove her out to the airport to catch her plane home. That night, however, Bill and Donna had a phone call from Ottawa. Mother had suffered some kind of emotional and mental breakdown during her flight and had had to be taken from the plane under sedation and be hospitalized. At the end of two years she was still showing only fleeting signs of recovery.

It was a difficult way to begin a marriage, but Bill and Donna were young and resourceful and loved each other very much, and they began to add to the comfort of their apartment. First they bought a canary, and then two small, very well-behaved dogs. The canary died. They went to a pet store and found another that looked exactly like the dead bird. Unfortunately it had already been sold, but they contacted the new owner and persuaded her to let them have it. One morning they got up to find the cage empty, though its doors were still closed and all the windows in the apartment screened. Nevertheless the bird was never found, not even a feather of it. Then the dogs began walking around something invisible in the middle of the room. When the dogs were left alone, Donna and Bill, on their return, would find them hiding under the bed or in a corner, whining. They had to be coaxed to come forward. One dog became so terrified that it never stopped shaking, even its sleep, and it was sent to a relative, where it soon fully recovered.

The TV stations at this period used to go off the air at 1 a.m., but the people immediately above and immediately below the apartment complained to Bill and to the landlord that the TV playing loudly at three in the morning disturbed them. They had heard loud conversations and what sounded like TV drama. Then they complained about all-night parties. These were loud and violent; things were knocked over; there was laughter and background music. Nevertheless, when they knocked on the door, Bill answered the knock clad in pyjamas, his hair tousled, obviously just woken from a sound sleep. After that there were complaints about an opera singer's practice sessions and her hours of singing scales and exercises. An opera singer had actually lived in the apartment at one time. (One often comes across houses where chanting, praying aloud and singing have occurred, and one wonders if this repetitious activity may set up vibrations that act as invocations to cause ghosts to collect.)

Bill left for work every morning at a quarter to seven, and Donna would snuggle down in bed for a few extra minutes of precious sleep. One day at five past seven she heard the fire door open with the usual popping sound, and footsteps coming down the hall and stopping at the apartment door. Thinking that it was Bill who had forgotten something and was unwilling to wake her, she rushed to the door. No one was there. This became a daily pattern, but only on the days when Bill was gone. He said he believed her story, and for a while she continued to open the door, but very soon those early naps became times of tension, waiting for the sound of the fire door opening and the approaching steps. She began to think, 'What if, some morning, there was someone or something there?' and she stopped going to the door. Having a girl friend stay overnight did not help the situation, for the steps occurred only when Donna was alone in the apartment. Once she got up very early and went out into the hall and hid behind the door, waiting for it to happen, but it never did.

Up till this time, apart from the incident with the car, the manifestations had been no more than a nuisance – nerve-racking, to be sure, but not physically dangerous. One morning, however, Bill and Donna awoke to find the electric stove turned on to the highest setting and the kitchen breathtakingly hot. Reason said they had forgotten to turn it off, but they had gone out for dinner the previous night and not used the stove. In the following week more and more electrical appliances were turned on – toasters, coffee-makers, kettles etc. One night Donna baked a pizza and placed it on the table and Bill began to eat. Donna nibbled on her salad, got up from the table and poured them both glasses of milk. Though Bill's portion of pizza was then cool enough to eat, Donna burned her lips so badly that she had to get medical help.

Bill was studying to be a detective, so his policeman's logic took over, and he conducted a methodical, logical and thorough examination. When all the logic had failed, they decided to try another route and a relative was asked to call Jean.

The apartment building was only five years old, and no other building had ever been erected on the site. Jean checked out the occupancy and discovered that apartment 308 and the apartments on each side of it were usually empty. This confirmed something that had been bothering Donna and Bill. They had gone to look at the apartment first on 8 January. The rent had been paid up to the end of the month, and yet nobody was living there, and they were able to move their belongings in ten days earlier than they had expected. This, moreover, was at a time when apartments were hard to find in the city.

Using their psychic abilities, Jean and her friends were able to contact the spirit of an elderly widow who had lived in a small cottage. The land on which the apartments were built had been an apple orchard, and she was pushed into this orchard each day in a wheelchair. She still claimed that the land was hers. The ghost-hunters talked to her, asked her to leave, told her that friends and family were waiting to take her to her new home. She left happily, telling them that her father and baby sister were there and that she wanted to be with them. They talked to Donna and Bill a few days later, and it appeared that the fire and heat problem had been solved but that the other manifestations continued.

Jean organized a seance the following week. Margaret and John from 'the house on the hill' were asked to attend. Margaret arrived in a weak condition, and John had to support her physically. He led her to a straight-backed chair, in which it took several minutes for her to regain her strength. She and John were wearing some extremely beautiful and valuable silver and turquoise Navaho jewellery. (They had spent a considerable amount of time in the American south-west, where the Navaho Indians lived.) As they joined hands for the seance, Margaret immediately slumped forward, her face resting on the table. After several minutes she straightened up, shook off the hands that held her on each side and slowly took off her jewellery, piece by piece, slamming one piece at a time in front of each person round the table – a ring to this one, a bracelet to that. Occasionally she snatched a piece back and replaced it with a different one. The force she used was tremendous, and Jean shuddered to think of the damage being done to the jewellery. Then she said, 'Hold or wear this! It is all you have to protect you!' She took a deep breath, stood up and stalked to the eastern window, stood for a moment and turned. The fragile British Margaret had become a large male North American Indian. A series of very vigorous arm gestures, deep guttural snarls and roars and some very intricate dance steps followed. Then she turned to the window and performed an elaborate ceremony to the setting sun. She turned, facing the company, closed her eyes, sighed, and when she opened her eyes she was Margaret once again, and she slid to the floor, her legs unable to support her. Everyone ran forward and picked her up and placed her in a chair.

Three-quarters of an hour later she had recovered sufficiently to tell the group that a foreign object, something of a very powerful magic, had been abused and misused, instead of being treated with respect. Donna and Bill looked at each other and turned white. 'Oh, my God, could it be ...?' and 'Do you think it is ...?' they said in unison.

Bill began to explain that the unusual wedding gift from his mother had been a large Chinese idol called Ho Tai, a money god. While they had thanked her, they had both immediately hated the thing. When asked if 'hate' was too strong a word to use, they both said No, that was exactly how they had felt. They had wrapped the god in old underwear and hidden him in a bottom drawer. Jean asked if they could see him, and Donna went to the bedroom and brought him out. His long ears were pierced; his open mouth had tiny, perfect teeth, and one hand clutched a bulging bag. The hands and face were very pale and appeared to be unglazed. His robe was a beautiful green with a yellow and dark blue pattern. Jean loved him immediately. 'He was wonderful,' she says. Everyone else, however, shared Donna and Bill's feelings; they hated him. Jean suggested that they should get rid of him and pointed out that he was extremely valuable and that they should sell him. They insisted that they couldn't. The consensus of the group was that the Ho Tai was the heart of the problem, however.

Jean suggested that he could be cleansed, rededicated and thoroughly reconditioned, and offered to bring over the necessary equipment and do what was necessary in the apartment. Again Donna and Bill refused and asked Jean to take the thing away and 'kill it'. Jean agreed to take it away and handed it to one of the men and asked him to carry it downstairs and place it on the sidewalk. Being inattentive, he took it to the elevator, and on each floor the people waiting for the elevator started to get in, then stepped back, muttering, 'I think I'll walk.' When Jean herself went outside, Ho Tai was sitting serenely on the sidewalk surrounded by an apprehensive group.

Jean said, 'Well, sir, you are homeless. Would you like to remain here or would you prefer to come home with me.' She then impressed upon him that she would tolerate no mischief and that he would have to behave. When Ho Tai arrived at his new home, he was bathed in sandalwood oil and immersed in sea-salt, and a quiet night was spent by all, including Donna and Bill, who slept late and woke to a world of difference. Calm and peace had reigned in their apartment, they told Jean, somewhat poetically, over the phone.

Jean is rather careful about her appearance and never goes anywhere improperly dressed. 'Therefore,' she says, 'you can imagine my horror at being found at 9.30 one morning wearing bedroom slippers, a coat over a housecoat, my hair uncombed, at the corner of Blanshard and Pandora driving to Chinatown to buy a goldfish for Ho Tai – not a real goldfish but one carved out of wood with a flowing fin and tails. Turning the car around, I drove home and said, "Don't ever try that again!" '

After constant oiling and bathing and respectful treatment and finally being placed on Jean's living-room mantel beside a pair of Foo dogs (also, fortunately, green and yellow), Ho Tai quieted down and lived a serene life.

Ho Tai's story was written up by several journalists and reporters, one of whom, when told to rub the god's tummy and ask for money, awoke the following morning to finds a $10 bill on her dresser. Her father growled, 'I remember I owed you the ten dollars, but I wish you would stop nagging me about it.' He had not owed her the money and she had not nagged him.

Jean tried not to use or abuse Ho Tai's gifts, but one morning, being more broke than usual, she rubbed his tummy with oil and said, 'Ho Tai, I'm going junk shopping and I need a little extra money.' On going to her securely locked car, she found on the driver's seat a torn piece of cotton tied in a knot. On opening the knot she discovered 97 cents. Jean says, 'I wonder what would have happened if I had said, "I need a lot of money"?'

Jean sent several messages to Donna and Bill offering to return the now pleasant gentleman, but they always politely but firmly said, 'No, thank you.' They may well have been wise, for one night Jean's friend Betty, after a few glasses of wine, decided that she was strong enough to handle Ho Tai. Betty and Ho Tai were driven to her home at about eleven in the evening. Ho Tai was wearing a very becoming red silk scarf with a beaded fringe. At three in the morning he arrived back at Jean's home in a taxi, accompanied by a very distraught Betty, who announced that her husband had left her, that her marriage was ruined and that it was all Ho Tai's fault. Shoving him into Jean's arms, she left in tears. Apparently the moment she had placed Ho Tai on her coffee table she and her husband had begun a no-holds-barred verbal attack on each other. Her husband had finally left, vowing never to return. However, when she herself returned home after delivering Ho Tai, he had come back, and he apologized and a reconciliation took place.

For several years Jean received Christmas cards and expressions of gratitude from Bill and Donna, and Ho Tai lived in her house for seven years. Then one day Jean took him to sell at a flea market. Jean says, 'If you live in Victoria and own a green Ho Tai and are having problems with your electrical appliances, perhaps you should call me.'

It may seem absurd to blame all these manifestations upon an inanimate object, but it must be understood that idols of this kind were created for quite specific purposes. Ho Tai, for example, was a money idol. A 'soul', usually a piece of Chinese writing, in calligraphy, often a blessing of some sort, would be placed inside the figure of the god. One couple travelling in Europe once bought a Ho Tai, placed him in a suitcase and carried him all over Central Europe and finally back to New York. They were constantly plagued by incredibly severe toothache. Back in New York they took Ho Tai to Chinatown and asked for information about him. They were told that this particular god had been created to prevent toothache, and when sitting on a shelf or mantelpiece, this was his purpose in life. However, when wrapped in underwear and locked up in a suitcase, he produced the opposite effect. When Jean read of this story, she felt encouraged to go home, remove the green felt from the bottom of Ho Tai and reach inside him, where she found, instead of a paper 'soul', a sliver of bone wrapped round and round with a long light-brown hair. She could have no idea when the bone and hair were placed there, or why, or what it meant.

After Jean's second visit Donna had gone to the library and among other books picked up several on witchcraft. One day she told Jean that after reading the books she realized that her grandmother and an uncle had very possibly been witches, for, she said, they did strange things. One of the things that made her think this possible was that her grandmother had many jars and bottles and glasses full of fat around the house in the way Rebecca Nurse had in the Salem Witch story. They were tucked away in corners, in the fridge, on shelves and almost everywhere.

Psychic abilities are often handed down from generation to generation, and the ancient belief in 'witch blood' was used by superstitious people to vilify or even persecute those whose fathers or mothers had shown healing powers or powers of precognition. It seems, however, that those who have psychic abilities, who are sensitives, are more vulnerable to psychic attack than are others, even though they are also more able to use their gifts in a positive fashion. Thus, while the main source of the trouble appears to have been the Ho Tai, Donna's difficulties may have been partly caused by her inheritance. It is also possible that, quite unconsciously, Bill's mother, who initially appears to have felt that this rather plain girl was no fit match for her son, may have presented her gift with feelings of resentment that caused both Donna and Bill not to appreciate it and to hide it away.

In cases of psychic disturbance there is rarely one simple answer to the problem. Most frequently there are multiple causes of psychic phenomena, though it is usually necessary to deal only with the main cause for the other ones to cease to be effective. Certainly in the case of the Ho Tai it may be significant that Bill's mother, shortly after presenting her gift, suffered a breakdown. It could be that she was troubled by guilt at what she had done. It could even be that she herself had given the Ho Tai her personal command by way of the hair and the bone, though this must remain no more than a wild speculation.

Curses are not always delivered intentionally. Feelings of anger and resentment can be planted quite accidentally in an object or gift. I myself came across a striking example of this phenomenon.

It began with Warren, my wife Sylvia's hairdresser. He told her that one of his customers, a woman, was in a terrible state of depression and had begun to feel that she was under some kind of curse. Did Sylvia think that Robin could do anything about it? I agreed to investigate the situation and see what I could do, and Warren's customer came to visit me one afternoon.

She was a woman in early middle age, quite attractive and

well-spoken. She sat on the very edge of the living-room couch, her knees pressed firmly together, and an expression of sadness upon her face. I offered her a glass of wine, which she accepted, sipping it nervously. I asked her about her problem. She told me she was a nurse and that it was her custom to rent a room with a family, sharing the kitchen facilities, rather than live by herself. She would get on well with the family for a week or two and begin to relax and feel at home, and then the family would 'turn against' her, and life would become so uncomfortable that she had to move on. This had happened over and over again.

Initially, of course, I thought of paranoia or at least some other type of neurosis, but I probed further. She was a single woman, then? Yes, she was a widow. She had been married three times. Her first husband had died; her second marriage had lasted only six weeks. Her third husband was an alcoholic, and he had died of cirrhosis of the liver. He being her most recent husband, I asked her about him. He had, I gathered, been a very emotional, indeed passionate man, and not long before he died he had given her a ring with the jocular comment, 'I'm putting my brand on you, my girl.'

'Do you still have the ring?' I asked, feeling that sudden twinge of excitement that comes when one intuits that one has at last discovered the heart of a problem.

'Oh, yes,' she said, 'I always wear it.'

'Give it to me,' I said, and she took it off her finger and handed it me. I took it in my left hand, and the energy it gave off was tremendous; it was as if I were holding a hot coal. I said, 'Would you let me keep this ring for a few days? I will give it back to you next week!'

I had expected resistance, or at least curiosity, but I received none. She agreed. Shortly afterwards she left, and already she was moving with a little more confidence. Whatever else I had done, I had given her hope.

I took the ring to my study and buried it in sea-salt. Normally twenty-four hours in salt is enough to 'ground' energies in an object, but this time I left it there until she came to see me again. She entered the house with a much lighter step than before, and she was smiling. She had not smiled at all during her previous visit. Once again she sat upon the couch, but this time she settled back into it and did not perch on the edge. I offered her a glass of wine, which she accepted and drank with pleasure. She accepted a second glass. She told me she was feeling much better. She said she was thinking of moving into an apartment of her own and perhaps taking some courses at the university. She said she thought she might take a trip and visit her daughter in Calgary.

I gave her back her ring and told her that it had been the cause of her problems but that it was now cleansed. I explained that her husband had not, in all probability, meant to curse her at all, but that he had been very possessive and that his wish to keep her for himself had planted itself in the ring and prevented her from having successful relationships with other people. I told her that she was obviously more than usually sensitive to psychic influences and that when she did get an apartment of her own she should give me a phone call and I would go around and check the place out and bless it. She agreed with a grateful smile.

She left the house with a positive spring in her step, and I never heard from her again. I assume she had regained so much confidence that she did not think it necessary to trouble me. I wondered a little how she had got on, and asked Sylvia to ask Warren about her. Warren said she was a regular customer, and she was looking just fine and was no longer depressed in the slightest.

Rings are often repositories and transmitters of psychic energy. Engagement and wedding rings are particularly likely to carry psychic imprints from their owners. If ever one buys a second-hand engagement or wedding ring, one should cleanse it in salt before wearing it. Of course, the energy field the ring possesses may be wholly beneficial. A happy marriage will produce a happy ring. Nevertheless, it is better to play safe.

One of Jean's experiences also centres upon a ring, though this one did not carry either a curse or a blessing. She and her family were living in a house on Hampshire Street, and they were very happy there. She says:

'The only time we became aware of any visitors "from beyond" was when we made renovations. At those times the scent of an old-fashioned perfume, sweet and powdery, would fill the house – I associated it with the 1940s. We always had a radio or a television playing when we smelt the perfume, because the house also produced a buzz or a hum which was nerve-racking, and we tried to drown it out. One day Sandy was working in the garden, and discovered a wedding ring. We placed it in a glass bowl on the mantelpiece, intending to return it to the daughter of the house's former owner.

'That night we were jarred out of our sleep by the sound of an explosion. It must have been a truly tremendous one to wake us, for a few weeks before, our car, which we parked in front of our house, had been completely destroyed by a drunk driver, and we had all slept through the sound of the crash. We got out of bed and checked the house but could find nothing out of place. The next day while dusting the mantel I found the glass bowl and the ring broken into dozens of tiny fragments, all lying in a space of less than three inches. An explosion as strong as that should have sprayed fragments across the room. This was the last manifestation that occurred in the house.'

Jean cannot explain the perfume, the humming noise or the shattering of the ring, but we feel that they may have been connected. It is possible that the woman of the house, who wore strong perfume, may have been disturbed by the renovations, may even have produced the sounds of a vacuum cleaner at such times when she felt that dust was being created. It is possible, too, that the ring, buried, or lost, in the garden, was a link which bound her to the house until it was recovered. Once it was recovered, she could leave, breaking her connection with the house and simultaneously, and dramatically, the ring which had bound her. Nobody will ever know the truth of it.

5

Restless Relics

In a number of cultures, when a man dies, all his personal and intimate possessions are either destroyed or buried with him. It has been stated that this is because he might need his weapons, his clothes, even his dog, in an after-life, but there is another explanation. The intimate possessions of a person have been subjected to the energy field of their owner, and they can either transmit that owner's energy to new owners or act as chains preventing the dead person from ever completely leaving his home. The home itself, of course, can also keep a person from moving on to another plane if he or she has felt passionately fond of it, as we have already seen in the cases of the house on the hill and the house on St David Street.

I came across a situation of this kind myself in Oak Bay. The house-owner was Dr Graham Mills, a psychiatrist of considerable reputation and a long-time resident of Victoria. At an evening gathering in my house he told me he was having problems. He rather thought he had a ghost. I asked for details. He told me that he was having trouble sleeping, which was unusual for him. The electric lights in the house often flickered or went on and off without explanation. The electric doorbell would often ring and, on answering the door, he would find nobody there. Very sensibly, he disconnected the doorbell, but it continued to ring. His telephone was also playing tricks. It would ring without reason, and it would even continue to ring when it had been connected to his answering machine and programmed to cut in to record messages after only one ring. This was not only irritating, it was dangerous, for a psychiatrist, of all people, must have a telephone that works.

I said that I would come round and look the place over. I could sense that something was uneasy in the house, and felt that it needed attention. I asked him to move a particularly vibrant painting from his bedroom to his study, as I felt that it was probably contributing to his insomnia. And I asked about the house's history.

He told me that it had been built by an elderly couple as their retirement home, as the place in which they intended to end their days. The next owners were also retired, and the husband was blind. Eventually he had been transferred to an extended care home, and his wife had lived on in the house alone, both while he was alive and after his death. Finally she too died, and Graham had bought the house from her estate. It was a house that had been filled with death and the anticipation of death.

I called Jean in to help me deal with this house, and Sylvia, Jean and I visited Graham one early evening. We wandered around the house, and Jean noticed a piece of paper stuck on the refrigerator. 'What's this?' she asked, and Graham said, 'I found it lying around when I came here, and I thought it was interesting, so I stuck it on the fridge.' It was a timetable of tasks to be done, by the home-help who had been coming daily, at first because the blind husband needed more care than his wife could give him, and later to help the wife herself. 'Get rid of it,' said Jean firmly, and he did so.

I then suggested that Jean and I should be left alone in the house for half an hour or so, and that Graham and Sylvia should go for a walk, as it was a fine, clear evening. Off they went, and Jean and I, not speaking to one another and taking different routes, walked through the house, each of us, in our own ways, blessing and comforting the place, telling it that the sadness was all gone and that vitality had returned. We also directed our thoughts to the old lady from whose estate Graham had bought the house. She, we felt, was still attached to her home. We ended in the kitchen, which we felt had been the focus of her life, and there we both spoke aloud and told her to go, and immediately we felt an easing of the atmosphere. I then stood in what was the geographical centre of the house and blessed it with comfort, warmth, happiness, addressing each point of the compass in turn. We knew that all was now well. When Graham and Sylvia returned, we told him that he should have no more trouble, and he reported later to me that he was having no more problems.

I cannot blame everything upon that list, of course, but it was certainly a contributory factor. The old lady's life must have centred very much upon the daily routine in her last years. The list of shopping to be done and chores to be performed was, indeed, a symbol of her life in the house.

The same kind of problem occurred with another and more complicated haunting. My friend Teresa, who orders the chaos of my manuscripts and transforms them into legibility, told me that her parents' house was haunted, or at least she thought so. 'I think we have a ghost,' she said. I asked for details. She said that one of the bedrooms was so unpleasant that she hated to enter it. Moreover, while she was watching TV in a room upstairs, the set would switch itself on and off and even change channels without human assistance. When she was alone in the house, she would often hear people walking down the stairs and opening the front door. On one occasion, while talking on the phone, she heard footsteps going towards the kitchen so distinctly that she told her caller that she was going to check, and to call the police if she did not return to the phone in a few minutes. There was nobody to be found.

The family often heard sounds of people moving about upstairs. Her father, Rolland, became so convinced that there were intruders one night that he turned out the light and sat on the stairs in the dark hoping to catch them, but the sounds did not occur again.

The basement was particularly unpleasant. Teresa's mother, Mimi, a fine artist, used the basement as a studio but had become unable to work there, the atmosphere was so depressing. On one occasion she had felt a nudge from an invisible person.

I said I would be glad to investigate, but Teresa was not sure that her parents would agree. I said, 'Well, if they ask me, I'll help.' In the meantime I told her to try the onion test on the bedroom. 'Cut an onion into quarters,' I said, 'and put a quarter in each corner of the room. The onion, in normal circumstances, just dries up as it does if you leave a cut onion out on the kitchen counter. But if it grows slimy or turns black, you know that something is wrong.' The onion turned black and slimy. Teresa said it looked like 'primeval ooze'. Something was wrong.

People develop affection for their ghosts; they become part of the household, and as long as they cause no trouble, they are regarded much as one regards familiar furniture or even a pet. I had the feeling that Rolland and Mimi felt that way about their own ghost, though Mimi was growing more and more bothered by being unable to use the basement. One evening, however, something a little more definite occurred. Rolland and Mimi were sitting on a settee before a low coffee table. In front of Mimi lay a file of papers. Without any warning the file rose gently into the air and floated the length of the table and settled down before Rolland. Rolland looked at Mimi. 'Don't say a word!' he told her, and they simply sat and looked at the file.

It may have been the floating file that decided them to ask for help. I called up Jean, and she joined Sylvia and me on a visit. We gathered new information. Teresa had been accused of arriving home very late and noisily and having disturbed her parents. She had not done so; in fact, she had gone to bed early, only to be woken herself by heavy footsteps stumbling up the stairs as if the owner were drunk. She thought it was her brother who had been out partying. She said that it was not her; it must have been Bob. 'Bob did not come home last night,' her father said. From time to time also several members of the family had seen a shadowy figure in the garden.

Jean and I asked if we might wander round the house, and we did so. Jean felt that, 'Upstairs you could almost hear poltergeist energy; it sort of hummed. The children were far too old to produce poltergeist effects, but the energy was still there. The basement was a horror. The toilet there, and the area around it, and the steps leading out to the garden were soaked in fear. I have rarely felt a fear so unrelenting.'

When we got upstairs again, Jean wandered off into the garden as I talked a little with Rolland and Mimi. She said that, 'The property had once been densely wooded, and indeed the woods still remained, stretching from the end of the garden up Gonzales Hill. Many trees had been cut down to facilitate the building of the house, but several huge trees had been left in the garden. I felt I should not have come into the garden from the back door of the house, but by the way of the door leading into it from the basement. Feeling a little silly, I went down the steps to the basement door, turned, stood there for a few minutes and then slowly came up the stairs and faced the garden.

'I walked to a large tree standing alone. With my back to it, I looked through two trees, framing three other trees with a stone slab in the centre of them. Walking forward to the doorway formed by the pillars of the two separate trees, I was able to see in a line beyond the three trees two more trees on the other side, further on. It was obviously a pattern that could be reversed – one tree, two trees, three trees, two trees and then three trees, two trees, one tree. It was too perfectly balanced to be an accident, yet I could not find a reason or a motive.

'I went inside and asked Robin if he would like to see the garden. He immediately went and stood with his back to the first tree and, using his cane, took a sighting. I said, "What does it mean?" He replied, "My dear, I don't really know."

'On our return to the house we asked Mimi and Rolland for a little history. The house had been built in 1924 for Ernest Colbeck, an estate agent. At that time the area was still thickly wooded, and he had had the area at the foot of Gonzales Hill cleared to build what became the first house on the street. It was clear that in organizing the clearance he had chosen to leave some trees not only standing but standing in a particular pattern. Jean and I tried to work out what principles the pattern had followed but, try as we might, we could not come up with anything. I suggested that Colbeck might have been associated with some occult or masonic order, for in the twenties these were flourishing, but that did not solve the problem. Nevertheless the trees were significant and we were particularly interested in the altar stone.

We asked Rolland about it.

'Oh,' said Rolland, 'we found that when we were digging the vegetable garden and we heaved it up and put it there ourselves. I don't know why there, exactly. We just didn't feel like lugging it any further.'

We asked for more details of the previous owner. He had had the house built for him by a British architect. This was a bonus. Usually one has to go through a whole list of previous owners to find out exactly where the trouble lies. It seemed clear that Colbeck was our man. This became even more certain when we learned that after his wife had died he lived alone in the house for many years and became extremely eccentric. He had not made use of the upper floors of the house at all but had made his home in the basement. When Rolland and Mimi moved into the house, they found nails hammered into the walls all over the place, as if he had eschewed any kind of cupboard or closet and hung all his possessions on the walls. The place was also cluttered with personal effects of no value – half-empty tins of boot-blacking, discarded tools and things of that kind. 'There's still stuff of his down there,' Rolland said. Jean and I looked at one another. 'Ah!' we said.

Mimi told us that when they bought the house the old man was still alive, at the age of ninety, but in hospital. His niece came from Toronto to oversee the sale and stayed in the house for a short time. Mimi said that the purchase of the house was not as straightforward as it might have been, for the old man was insistent that whoever became the new owner must be fond of trees, must be someone who would take care of them. Mimi could say wholeheartedly that she loved trees, and that was satisfactory. They bought the house, and the niece made no difficulties. Indeed, she was in a hurry to get back to Toronto and was totally uninterested in any of the personal belongings her uncle had left in the house. Shortly after Rolland and Mimi moved in, the old man died.

The first step to take was very clear. We advised Mimi and Rolland to go through the basement and take out everything personal that the old man had left behind him. There was a shaving brush, shaving soap, various other toilet articles and some miscellaneous tins of boot-polish and things of that kind. We said, 'Either give the stuff away to a charity shop or put it in the garbage, but get it out of the house.' They followed our instructions, and a few days later Teresa told me that the atmosphere in the basement had markedly improved, but it still felt rather unpleasant. We then arranged a time for us to visit the house and deal with the problem more thoroughly. We said they could join us if they wished, but they said they preferred to leave us on our own to do what must be done.

One day at around noon Jean and I went to the house. Clearly there were three areas that needed special attention. First of all we tackled the bedroom, and I blessed the house. On the main floor I also delivered blessings, paying particular attention to the hall and the bathroom, which were directly above one of the trouble spots in the basement. We decided that the unpleasantness in the bedroom and on the main floor was due to emanations from the basement, and so down we went.

The atmosphere was much improved already. The removal of the old man's collection of old tins and bottles and miscellaneous toilet articles had helped a good deal. We circled the basement, not speaking very much to one another except for occasional comments. Jean used salt to ground the disturbing energies, and I blessed all the various areas, banishing bad memories and emotions. I had brought a pocketful of white pebbles with me, and I placed them in different parts of the area to act as transmitters of feelings of comfort and peace. I felt that, since I was taking away so many sources of negative energy, I must replace them with positive sources. One should never take away any energy field or source of energy without replacing it.

As I continued my work, Jean wandered out into the garden. She says:

'I set a chalice filled with water on the stone in the centre of the three trees, together with an incense-burner to represent the element of fire and of air, and a bowl of salt to represent earth. Leaving these there for the garden to grow accustomed to them, I returned to the basement. Robin had been working very hard, and the environment was much more bearable. I tried to break the space up into small areas. One that was devoted strictly to storage I charged with protection and safety. A workshop area was charged with stamina and safety. A cleaning area was easy, and a corner where there was a table for doing jigsaw puzzles was then taken care of.

'The area Mimi used for painting was not yet approachable, and the lavatory area and the area round the back door were still very much contaminated with fear. Robin said that the old gentleman had lived in this unpleasant area near the end of his life in the house; while it offered easy access to the garden, it was impossible to understand why a cultured person would choose to spend time here. Robin suggested fear as a motive. The lights would not be seen from the street, and the house would look completely deserted. Robin concentrated on this area. Using sound and rhythm he frequently struck the ground with his staff. As he worked, the light began to change, and with a final motion of his hand he turned to Mimi's working area and said, "Well, that's done. I'm going outside".'

I should interject here that I am giving Jean's recollection of my own actions and statements because, when I am working in this fashion, I operate very largely by intuition and therefore do not always remember clearly what I did or said; I do what feels necessary. I do remember clearly, however, the pain and fear amounting to anguish that I sensed in the small lavatory, and I knew that the old man had spent a great deal of time there. In all probability he was suffering from either incontinence or bowel troubles in his later days. In Mimi's working area it was not so much a feeling of fear that was dominant as a feeling of hopelessness, a negative dark fog of futility; this accounted for her inability to work imaginatively in that area, and I dispelled that gloom with some very strong, positive energies, continuing until I myself felt able to sense a confident happiness. The whole basement now felt warmer, and both Jean and I commented on this. Now it was time to tackle the garden.

We went into the garden by way of the basement door, feeling as if we were treading in Colbeck's footsteps, each of us following our own intuitions. One of the reasons for working in pairs is that, if there are two people working, one of them is likely to pick up energies and vibrations the other may miss; moreover, as no two people work in exactly the same fashion, it means that a couple can create what might be called a pincer movement, attacking from two directions at once.

According to Jean, I led the way. She says, 'I followed him and, using his staff, he followed the underground water line, although he insists he has no talent as a water witch. He had not been with me on the previous occasion when I had been shown where the water line had been laid. He walked the whole length of the water line. It was amazing. At each corner of the garden he pronounced a blessing, and then joined me at the stone we both called the altar.'

At the altar I remembered how important the trees had been to the old man who had organized them so carefully into a pattern, and I spoke to him, telling him that he need no longer worry about their health or safety. He need no longer watch over them. I concentrated my energy upon the altar stone between the trees and sent him a message to leave this place and go to the next plane. I used the soaring height of the trees to send him soaring up and away to his new life.

When I had done this, I watched Jean. She says, 'The land now having been cleansed of all spiritual impurities, I quickly performed a small ceremony over the burning incense. I then poured the burning incense on the stone, covered it with salt, then washed it back into the earth with the water.'

Places and land that have been inhabited by ghosts and spectres are suspended in a sort of limbo. The sacred elements that are poured back into the earth after a ceremony are the spiritual equivalent of yeast that, added to an appropriate brew, causes renewed fermentation. Everything comes back to life, and the energy of the earth begins to bubble again.

The atmosphere of the place did indeed begin to bubble. We wandered around the garden, both feeling strangely happy. We even found ourselves giggling and making jokes, and when we at last said farewell to the house, we knew it was in good shape.

We also felt a great deal of happiness for Colbeck, who was now released from his bondage. Jean, talking over his difficulties, said she knew with absolute certainty that the old gentleman had been intimidated by a young man who worked in the garden and that he had been rightly apprehensive about his safety. An even stronger fear, however, had been that acquaintances would call and he would be found incapable of hospitality or of caring for his home. His fear of humiliation caused him to become a recluse, spending his early mornings in the garden and his days hiding in the basement.

Teresa told us, after a few days, that the house was transformed. The bedroom was no longer depressing, there were no more steps on the stairs, and the television behaved normally. Moreover, and most cheering to us, she reported that the basement felt good enough for Mimi to work there once more.

6

The Indian Inheritance

If a bar of iron is subjected to a magnetic field in a certain fashion, it becomes itself a magnet, and a similar process occurs if a place is subjected to intense psychic energy over a period of years. One might say that the earth has a memory bank; it stores energies and emotions, and people who build upon rich-memoried earth often find themselves burdened with images and traumas of the past.

Sometimes a particular place rich in memory is recognized as being a place of strange power, and legends and stories grow up around it, the stories being less accurate accounts of history than ways of stating that the place should be treated with caution. Superstitions grow up around such places; these almost always express something of man's longing for certain powers that are classed as supernatural. Thus a well or a tree is credited with healing properties, a pool is said to grant precognition to those whose look into it, and there are places one must not visit by night or when the moon is full, for fear of disaster or even death.

One place on Vancouver Island that has this kind of reputation is Mystic Spring in the Cadboro Bay area of Victoria. The story goes that when Sir James Douglas in 1843 discovered Cadboro Bay, which he named after his brig, he was met by friendly natives, and he followed them through giant oak trees to a huge maple with a bright, sparkling spring at its foot. The water was as cold as ice in both summer and winter. The natives were convinced that it possessed magical properties. If a woman should look into the water when the moon was full, she would see reflected in it the face of the man who loved her. If a man looked into it, similarly, he would see the face of the woman who loved him and would marry him if he asked her. If a woman were barren and drank of the water, she would bear many children. The maple tree was a god who protected the spirit of the spring. As long as the tree stood, the water would creep to its feet for protection and shade. Cut down the tree, and the spring would come no more.

The young people of Victoria used to visit this spring to picnic, and when the moon was full, they would look into the water to see who were to be their future mates. On 21 April 1868 Miss Julie Booth was found drowned in the spring. Twenty years later the maple, called Father Time because of the long beards of Spanish moss hanging upon it, was massacred, and the mystic spring dried up and was not seen for many years.

When Jean first came to Victoria, she heard many stories about Mystic Spring and talked to people who had visited it as children and had celebrated their high school graduation by picnicking at the spring. One day, Jean says, 'A Mr Jones phoned me to say that his house was disturbed and his wife was very distressed. Could I come and visit it? And, by the way, he owned the Mystic Spring. Of course, I couldn't resist.

'The house was lovely and the back yard was a green jungle around a deep, sparkling, clear pond. At one end stood a slim young maple, a young nymph instead of the old Father Time that it had replaced. Apparently the former owner had found a small seedling maple and had cleared away the surrounding weeds, and as the tree grew, a damp spot had appeared beside it, and together tree and spring grew and flourished. My attention wandered to the pool, as I tried to concentrate on the lady and the house.

'Born in Britain, she was a professional entertainer. Since the recent death of her mother she had grown increasingly depressed. Not long before my visit she had seen her mother's face reflected in a mirror. This, I think, was significant, for the spring had also been used as a mirror. She thought that the spirit of her mother, who had always been jealous of her career, was trying to possess her body and to take over her life, her career and her marriage. Try as I might, I could not feel that I could help her in any way. I gave her some good advice, of the rather standard positive-thinking variety, but felt that I was not getting through to her and could not help at all. Finally one day, after she phoned me to tell me she was growing a wart on her nose, exactly where her mother had had one, I introduced her to a British medium and her husband, and although I never heard from her again, I gathered that they had begun a friendship that was comfortable for all concerned. I came to the conclusion that the lady was more interested in the drama of her situation than in anything else, and really wanted a fortune-teller, not an exorcist.

'Two strange things happened during my investigation of the house. I took a sample of the water to Priscilla Bethel, whose expertise as a dowser and analyst I had made use of several times, and asked her if, by using radiosthesia, she could trace the source of the water. Holding a pendulum, first over the water and then over the map, she immediately said, 'Why, this is from Mystic Spring.' I'd also asked for a sample of the mint growing by the spring and was given an armful. The plants were over six feet tall, and the individual leaves were at least a foot long. I separated my armful into small bundles and tried to dry them. Air-drying, dehydration and even pressing in an old-fashioned flower press were no use. The mint always turned into a disgusting black slime.'

Several years later, just across the highway from Mystic Spring, a young family turned a garage into a tiny, perfect Russian Orthodox church. Jean's young son, Kord, became an altar boy and attended the church for some years. The small congregation could not support the church financially, so the young priest worked the night shift at a local hospital. One morning he went home to discover his wife, the mother of his two little girls, dead. Like the first woman, she had felt the atmosphere of the house and the neighbourhood intolerably depressing, and had told Jean about it. The overflow from

Mystic Spring, which was by then no longer a small freshet but a very considerable pond, almost a small lake, had trickled under the street and through their garden.

Jean felt very badly about the almost offhand way in which she had treated the other woman's depression, for now it seemed that there had been something extremely serious about it. Two women living on land containing the waters of the Mystic Spring had suffered extreme depression. It is not wise for people of other strong races or religions to build or live on land held sacred by another race. Indeed, the consequences of doing so can be extremely disturbing and even life-threatening. Jean and I came across just such a situation in December 1976.

It began at a pre-Christmas party at Sandra's house. Jean remembers it vividly. She says that when Sandra opened the door to let her in, 'I was aware of an instinctive movement by the fireplace. A very beautiful red-haired young lady turned and walked directly towards me with her hands outstretched. "I know you," she said, though we had not met before.'

The young woman, who said her name was Stancy, told Jean that she had a problem, and asked if they could find a quiet place to talk. She was a teacher and the mother of two little girls, and she and her husband owned and were living on property that had once belonged to the infamous Brother Twelve.

Brother Twelve had been the leader of a group of people who had settled to form a community on Cedar Point, on the east coast of Vancouver Island in 1977. The group had its own somewhat mystical religion, which appears to have owed much to Theosophy but something also to the views of Ouspensky and Gurdjieff. It was devoted to the principle of manual labour as a way of achieving spiritual purity, and all the men, women and children were made to work very hard indeed. Brother Twelve, a Messianic figure, kept all the money that his disciples contributed, and some of them contributed a great deal. After some time he was joined in his running of the community by a woman who called herself Lady Zee and who was clearly a sadist. Women in an advanced state of pregnancy were made to perform back-breaking tasks. The whip was used not infrequently.

The community retained its headquarters on Cedar Point but moved much of its activity onto the nearby islands of Valdez and de Courcey, partly in order to escape the attention and the increasing disquiet of the citizens of Nanaimo, the nearest town. The community became almost a slave camp; indeed, the members of it had neither money nor rights and were treated exactly as if they were slaves, until, in 1933, the movement disintegrated and Brother Twelve and Lady Zee disappeared, together with the community's money, and were never heard of again.

The land upon which Brother Twelve had settled was already rich in memories, and, interestingly enough, those memories included slavery, for the Kwakiutl Indians who had a village on Cedar Point were slave-owners. Slaves who had to be discarded for one reason or another were killed and their bodies were thrown out into the bush behind the village to be eaten by predators and to rot. The senior members of the tribe were treated differently. Their bodies were placed in boxes in the trees on Valdez Island, which was the tribe's ritual burying-ground.

Cedar Point and the islands of Valdez and de Courcey were sometimes also the scenes of inter-tribal battles, for the Haida from the north would from time to time make Viking-like raids from their homeland of the Queen Charlotte Islands and attack the coastal villages of Vancouver Island.

Brother Twelve had thus founded his community of mysticism and enlightenment in a place almost calculated to pervert his original intentions. A group engaged in frequent meditation will always pick up the energies of a place more easily than others, and it seems not unlikely that the long history of Indian ritual killings and feastings accounted in part for the way in which Brother Twelve's initially peaceful and gentle community became a place of cruelty, torture and even murder.

Stancy knew of Brother Twelve but believed that, being pure of heart and working hard and having a positive attitude, she and her husband were strong enough to overcome any environmental problem. They were wrong. Almost immediately the children were affected. They began to display new and vicious attitudes towards their toys and the family animals. Once Stancy discovered a kitten tied up, and spoke to the children in horror. The children shook their heads and were upset; they asked their mother why *she* had tied up the kitten. The family became accident-prone. One girl tripped on her shoelace, fell on a hidden piece of glass and had to be taken to hospital for her wound to be repaired with many stitches. Pets disappeared without trace. Footsteps sounded outdoors at night. Stancy and her husband suffered from a constant feeling that they were being spied upon. Unpleasant dreams afflicted them, and often appeared to come true. None of the vegetables they planted grew properly; they were weak or stunted or failed to come up at all. Her husband had an accident with a saw while cutting wood.

Lately she had dreamed of a date, 22 January, on which her husband would be killed in his truck on a quiet country road along which he drove every day. She knew that if she told her husband he would insist on driving that road on that particular day, whether he needed to or not. She thought of disabling the truck or of going out and leaving him baby-sitting and unable to leave the children, but she felt that that would simply be postponing the inevitable. She believed that the problem was the land and its history. It was crying out for blood. The evil was in the earth itself, and she had to find a way to cure it.

Jean, Leon Reed and I met in Jean's house to discuss this situation. We felt that a great deal of power would be needed to counteract the effects of so much past cruelty and bloodshed, but we could not work out exactly how to formulate an exorcism. For a number of reasons, we could not manage an on-site ritual. The winter weather, our own schedules and the presence of an apparently sceptical husband and two young children made that impossible. Apart from this, Leon's mode of working was not the same as Jean's, and I myself at that time had not taken part in a formal exorcism and felt, inwardly, that I would do better if I worked in my own way. Jean felt the same. We therefore decided that we would work separately, but at exactly the same time, thus sending three strong waves of energy from three different and, we trusted, complementary points of view.

At nine o'clock on the evening of 22 January 1977 we each performed our own rituals, and, oddly, we never told each other exactly what we did. I myself went to my desk in my study, cleared it of all irrelevant objects, laid out symbols of the elements, lit a candle and began the ritual, working not from a book but intuitively. You might say I was ad-libbing. I spoke the words aloud and, indeed, at certain points very loudly – so much so that, when my daughter Alison returned home with a friend some time after I had begun, the friend asked her nervously who was that shouting in the next room. 'Oh,' said Alison, 'it's only my Dad doing a spell!' I do not know whether or not her friend was much reassured.

I concentrated my attention not upon Brother Twelve but upon the energies left behind by the earlier period. I perceived the Cedar Point farm as part of a whole area that needed to be cleansed. Therefore I saw the water connecting the Indian burial ground on Valdez to de Courcey and the mainland as being significant, and, because water itself always conducts psychic energies, I concentrated upon that element.

Although I tape-recorded the words, I spoke so that I had a record of my part in the cleansing of Cedar Point. A transcript of everything I said would be extremely tedious. On such occasions one repeats key words and commands over and over again to hammer them home, as it were. Even a truncated version would be hard to take. Therefore I will summarize.

I began by addressing the Goddess and asking for strength and power, 'the power of love, the strength of love, the strength of light, the power of light'. I directed the 'light' and the 'power' into Stancy, to make her the source of all the healing. I asked for the release of the earthbound spirits, saying, 'Release these spirits from their prison; release them from the earth, the water.' I asked for purification of the water and of the air above it. I asked for healing and purification of the memories of the spirits, and I sent healing light into the trees, the plants, the animals, the house and the people in the house. I asked that light should burn through all the chains that held the spirits to this place, and

I asked for release and healing for all who had suffered. I concluded with an assertion,

> … and the light is spreading, spreading,
> it is touching all the people,
> releasing, healing all the people.
> The place is now a place of light.
> A place of light.
> And it is done.

As this last fragment shows, I spoke rhythmically, not merely because I am used to writing verse but because I was dealing with a culture not only devoted to but centred upon rhythmic dance and speech. To talk in carefully poised and unrhythmical sentences would be, I felt, like talking English to a francophone; while the intent of the message, the thrust of it, would be felt, it would be resented and would have no authority.

Jean took a different approach to the problem and concentrated not upon the Indian tenure of the land but upon the legacy of Brother Twelve. She says:

'I did a meditation ahead of time, casting myself in spirit form upon the land to look it over, and I felt the husband and wife were all right, but I was really worried about the children, mainly because, although Brother Twelve had built a school and had furnished it right down to chalk and blackboard and textbooks, he had refused anyone except Alma, his consort, the right to have children. I felt that these children were very definitely at risk, by living on property where he did not wish them to be.

'I stood quietly, using breath control, and centred myself. Then I used the ancient method of energizing and cleaning my whole body that is called "chakra cleansing". Basically this means that one concentrates on the energy centres of the body and step by step breathes out all obstructions and impurities. The technique is used by student practitioners of Yoga. After I had done all this, I sent my psychic energy through the solar plexus chakra to my feet to ground me, to my hands to help me project energy and heal, and to my third eye to enable me to see clairvoyantly, and to travel astrally if it should be necessary.

'Now that my physical body was centred and grounded and my astral body was free of all contamination, I said the words: "I dedicate myself and my work to my Lady, the great and gracious Goddess." I asked for all helpful forces of nature to draw nigh and to aid me in my work, and using a map of the area for an altar cloth, I surrounded the whole property with a ring of salt.

'I took one white candle in a candle-holder and said: "I light this white candle and place it at the east. O wind of the east, blow wildly across this land blowing away all contamination from angry words or expressions, from blows, from blustering, from blame, from pain, from injuries and from all harm and wickedness." Then I placed the candle in the east.

' "I light this candle and place it in the south. O fire of the south, burn away all the contamination on this land, burn away all sorrow, all unjust acts. Resurrect from cremation all attempts to destroy evidence; blow away all acts to suppress the truth." I placed the candle in the south.

' "I light this candle to the waters of the west. O waters of the west, flow over the land, float free the contamination from emotional distress, release all memory of memories of pain, sorrow, torture and revenge." This candle I placed to the west.

' "I light this candle to the earth of the north. O earth of the north, give up all contamination from barrenness, from internment; resurrect all secrets and treasure buried in the earth; give up all wickedness and unhappy memories." This last candle I placed to the north.

'I repeated these words until the emotions were gone. Then I swept up all the salt and placed it in the water. I heated the water over a candle and blew on and fanned the water to cause ripples. This water I placed in the centre of the map. Then I took the candle of the east: "Let the winds blow pure and clear over this land." I put out the candle and said, "Welcome and protect all who dwell here."

'I took the candle from the west and said, "Let your water be clean and pure, and bring forth life from the land." I put out the candle and said, "Welcome and protect all who dwell here."

'I took the candle from the north: "Candle of the north, earth be rich and fruitful. Welcome and protect all who live upon your bounty." Then I put out the candle, and I poured the salt and water into the earth element.

' "Thank you all helpful and friendly spirits. Return now to your own abode and harm none on your way. This is my wish, and as I wish, so must it be.

' "Blessed Lady, thank you for your presence and aid.

' "Blessed Be!"

'I then realized that at some time during this ceremony I had torn a three-cornered hole in my robe.'

Leon's account of his part in this exorcism runs as follows:

'I was sharing an old house on Vista Heights in Victoria in those days. I was known to almost everyone as "Patches", a nickname reflecting the state of my clothing. My income was at that time "fashionably" lean. Jean and I had talked about the need to work on this particular project the week before. We were teaching a mediumship development class once a week at her Oak Bay home. I knew a little about Brother Twelve from a book about him written by his brother, but I had never been able to go to the island where he had lived. Yet a further obstacle to the work was our inability to find a time when we could all work on this together. So it was decided that each of us would work on it separately.

'I felt I had a link to the subject of the work in that I had met the lady who occupied the land. As I recall, she and I had met at Jean's when she had come to tell about the difficulties at her island property. I think we may have also gotten a letter; however, I cannot find it, so I'm not certain.

'On the evening we had agreed to, I put on my robe of hand-dyed cotton and set up the living-room as a temple. I placed the main altar in the east, making sure I had everything. The symbolic elements, a pair of candles for fire, a chalice of water, incense for air, and salt in a saucer for earth. My magical dagger which would be used to open the circle and banish unwanted influences completed the tools for that night.

'I began with an altar consecration, purifying the individual elements and charging them to further purify all that they touched. I then performed the middle pillar exercise, a centring meditation in a ceremonial magick tradition in which one balances the forces within oneself, gaining contact with one's angelic protectors. I trod barefoot upon my circle of cloth, drawn to my own design of alternating pillars of light and dark with the twelve banners of the name emblazoned in Hebrew on their capitals, each name a tetragram, or four-lettered name, standing for one of the twelve signs of the zodiac or one of the twelve tribes of Israel. Next I performed the banishing ritual of the pentagram, drawing up my circle of protection. This process is derived from the medieval methods of ceremonial magic and casts a circle of blue fire about the performer, with flaming five-pointed stars emblazoned in the four directions. Within these stars reside the angelic beings of Raphael in the east, Michael in the south, Gabriel in the west, Auriel in the north. These angelic beings protect and defend the circle as well as witness the work and give warning of approaching danger, like guards in a watchtower.

'Having the temple established fully, I seated myself in the centre of the circle and focused on the object of the work. I could feel myself travel out of my body in my astral form towards the woman I had met. I had earlier consulted a map to see just where this place was. Never having been there, it took a little while to locate her. Finally I made my connection. I could picture her face. When I was sure I had the right place, I knew I could proceed. I had chosen to face west for the meditation, as the work of the evening concerned the dead. The west being guarded by Gabriel, Angel of Judgement, I had asked that Gabriel assist me to purify this woman's land of the influences cast by those previously living there. I had been seated in the lotus position, and upon finishing this little prayer I tried to rise. I got my foot caught in the hem of my robe as I lurched up and heard the sound of tearing fabric.

'I returned to the eastern altar and recentred myself. This was to settle myself down before proceeding. Peace came over me, so I turned again to the west with my ritual knife. I took care always to move in a sunwise or clockwise direction. Again I followed the astral thread of connection to the island home of our somewhat unsettled friend.

'I recall that I made some address to the west stating that I wanted to put to rest whatever disruptive force was residing there. I asked Thoth, the Egyptian god of learning, the ibis-headed one, to assist me by providing me with the information I needed to do this.

'It was at this point that I realized I was not alone in the work. Though I was physically the only one in the house, I could feel the familiar presence of Jean, and then a few moments later Robin.

'Shortly thereafter I felt the need to begin the banishing work. For me it started as a dance and a song, building upon itself in a spinning, bliss-filled cone. The words came naturally and went somewhat as follows:

'Energies, phantoms of yesterday,
Ground yourself when I say.
Bother not the living souls,
Rather pursue your higher goals.
Travel now towards the light,
And give up your pain tonight.
Blessings on the haunted earth,
Dissolve this pain and fear in mirth.
Cleansing salt and sacred sound,
Banish evil from this ground.
By tangled grove and twisted tree,
And by my will so mote it be.

'After this I broke free of the cone and sent it astrally to its goal. I fell to earth, eyes closed. I could feel the power go and after a while arrive at its destination and merge into the land.

'I remained upon the floor, body akimbo like a rag-doll. I felt drained but good and safe. I knew that it would work but that it might be a while before the banishment was fully effective.

'I then closed the rite, thanking the gods and angels for their assistance and presence and asking that they return to their realms with my blessing.

'Later Jean and I would compare notes and find that we shared many of the same feelings that night.'

Jean adds a footnote: 'The following day I phoned Robin and Leon; we had all been delayed about five minutes in starting our ceremonies; we had all worn the colour purple, and each of us had torn our clothing during the ceremony.'

An immediate improvement of spirit occurred to Stancy and her family; their morale improved and there were no bad dreams. The car accident did not occur. Nevertheless, this was still far from being the ideal place in which to live, and after six months or so they left the farm and moved elsewhere.

It is not easy to 'cleanse' land that has a rich history of emotional disorder or of ritual. One may improve the situation, but one cannot always do much more than that. Moreover, it is also difficult to discover whether or not a piece of land has, in the far past, been used for ritual purposes. The history of the Indian culture and of the settlements and sacred places of the Indians on Vancouver Island is a book that has not yet been written. Had that book been written, Jean might have understood the problems of Mr and Mrs Peters a little sooner.

Mr Peters was in real estate, and Mrs Peters was in communications, working for a local radio station. Jean had met her several times while being interviewed on her radio show. One day she visited Jean for tea and sympathy. Seven years earlier her husband had found his dream house. It was too expensive for them to buy at that time, but it became a yardstick for them, and they measured each house they saw against it, and each financial gain against the cost of purchasing it. Every house they owned was measured against this perfect house. Regularly, every three years, the house was sold, and one year earlier they had at last been in the financial position to buy it.

From the moment they moved in, problems that had previously seemed minor suddenly exploded into full-fledged catastrophe. Their two teenaged children were very unhappy, and both left home almost immediately. When Mr and Mrs Peters drove to work, they always stopped on the way to have breakfast, because their own kitchen equipment was still in boxes, and they stopped somewhere for dinner on the way home. Each evening they intended to unpack the boxes, but never did so, and a year after they had moved into the house the kitchen they had thought perfect was still in disarray, and they had rarely eaten more than a snack in the house.

Mrs Peters' career accelerated. New opportunities presented themselves, and she won awards for her work on radio. As her reputation grew, so did her self-confidence. Mr Peters, however, was exhausted. He enjoyed working in the yard and formulated great plans but never seemed able to accomplish any of them. Mrs Peters frequently found him asleep in his lawn chair. He seemed to hate coming into the house and would stretch out his time in the garden until as late in the day as possible, sometimes until well after dusk. The dream house that was to shelter them and provide a social background for their lives remained undecorated, with boxes still unpacked. Two Christmases came and went with no celebration. No tree was ever put up and decorated, although one year they did buy one, only to leave it in the back yard. Birthdays were celebrated in restaurants. Everything relating to the house was too difficult, too much effort to do. At work both were successful and productive; it was only at home that their lives and their marriage were a failure.

After hearing this story Jean suggested that the practical solution to the problem would be to sell the house and get something much more convenient. The Peters did not need as much space as they had, and both of them spent a good deal of time in travelling. The house was obviously not making them happy. The Peters, not surprisingly, were unconvinced, and at their request Jean and her friends went out to investigate the house. Doug Thomas, a local healer, drove the car and, much to Jean's relief, he got lost as she herself so often does on her first visit to a haunted house.

Jean discovered that the house stood opposite one of Victoria's most noted tourist attractions, and was surprised that she had not been told of this when she had been given directions to find the place. The house inside proved to be depressing, boring, uninspiring. Doug did a brief tour of the rooms and went into a basement room to meditate.

Later the four people met in the living-room for a discussion. Jean looked over at Mr Peters and, she says, 'He appeared to age before my eyes. I said, "You have aged ten years in the eighteen months you have lived in this house." He said "Nonsense!" His wife and daughter said, in unison, "Yes, he has!" and showed us a photograph of a healthy young man taken on the day they had moved in.'

Jean said, 'Please. Sell the house, because if you don't, you will die.' She comments: 'I had never said such a thing to anybody before in my life, and was very upset at myself for saying anything so stupid. Using logic, he explained the financial reason why it would be to their disadvantage. I replied, "Which is more important – your money or your life?" '

Since he himself had been the real-estate agent responsible for selling the house each time it had changed hands, Jean asked him for its history. The house had been sold to middle-aged couples each time, and each time the man's health had deteriorated. The men spent long hours in the garden, and each one had died after a massive heart attack, one in the garden and the others in the house. Until they moved into the house, the women had appeared to be interested only in the house and family, but they were forced by their husbands' illness to take on more and more responsibilities. The women became stronger and more effective as the men declined in health and efficiency. Even after appreciating this background to their problems, the Peters remained adamant that they could not afford to sell the house.

Jean felt that more information was necessary, and she and Doug left the house, promising to keep in touch. Several weeks later Mrs Peters phoned to say that a lady in a neighbouring house had drowned herself in the shallow stream that flowed through both their properties. She had been despondent after the death of her husband from a heart attack in the garden. Mr Peters had decided to sell.

In due time the house was sold and the Peters bought an apartment in town without any yard. Each of them survived professionally, but the marriage ended.

The house was bought as a wedding present for a young couple attending university. Jean worried about the new owners, but it was difficult to intervene. Were they to be told the house's history, it might destroy their hopes of a happy life. Moreover, if one tells someone that their house is, or has been, haunted, they begin to dwell upon the matter and may even create a receptive atmosphere for hauntings that might not otherwise occur. Ghosts do, after all, leave houses without any urging from time to time, and it is clear that some people are more vulnerable than others to psychic disturbance. Indeed some people appear to be totally unaffected by atmospheres which distress others unbearably. There is, too, the ethical question. Has one the right to intrude. Is it possible to do so either gracefully or effectively? In the present climate of opinion it is more than likely that anyone who told a householder that the house had ghosts would be regarded as crazy or, at the very least, resented. Moreover, people have different religious beliefs, and these are important to them and are their emotional and spiritual anchors; one should not disrupt a strong and settled faith by presenting views of the spiritual world which conflict with it and might lead to a distress far more debilitating and harmful than any but the most formidable haunting.

The haunting of this house was, however, clearly formidable, and several years later Jean discovered the probable cause. She was doing some research on that area of Victoria and turned up evidence that this particular piece of land had been used by native Indian women as a retreat following childbirth. They took their newborn there to recuperate and to become strong and healthy. Men were not permitted on the place. Now the women who live in the place with the men become strong and healthy, and the men become weak and die, affected by the ancient taboo.

The house at present looks unkempt and ill-cared-for; the paint is peeling and the hedge is untrimmed.

Once again we are faced with a power spot, and perhaps we have no right to tamper with it. It belongs to the spiritual world of the native people, and we are interlopers. This place was, and remains, a place of power and a religious site. It is to be hoped that in the fullness of time the house will be bought and inhabited by a woman or women who have no intention of marrying. It would suit them perfectly.

7
Point Ellice Ghosts

Sometimes there are connections between hauntings. Several houses may be affected by the same or similar phenomena, often because they have been built in an area which has, for one reason or another, become receptive. The houses on the banks of the Selkirk Water portion of the Gorge waterway in Victoria may be of this kind. There are, in fact, very few houses there now; the area on both sides of the Point Ellice Bridge is largely industrialized. Nevertheless, two of the houses came to Jean's attention, and though they presented quite different case histories, there was one phenomenon common to both of them.

The first house was on Raynor Avenue, on the bank of Selkirk Water beside Point Ellice Bridge and just about opposite Point Ellice House. Clare, who was renting the house, met Jean and Tara several times to discuss the various phenomena she had encountered. One of these was a red light that moved slowly along the banks of the Gorge about eighteen inches above the ground. There was no physical explanation for it. The house was often afflicted with strange noises – creaks and rappings and sighs.

One night, as Clare was holding a Tupperware party, the company had been startled by a tremendous blow upon the side of the house, as if the whole length of it had been slapped by the cudgel of a giant. This totally terrified the party in the living-room and they all ran into the street and called to a man nearby, who investigated and found no sign of anything untoward. At last, too scared to return to the house, they took their party up the street to another house and held it there. Jean felt that any ghost that would take on a whole Tupperware party deserved and demanded to be investigated.

Jean and Tara arrived after dark at the house, which brooded behind a straggly hedge and displayed only one lit window upstairs, reminding Jean of the cover pictures of popular gothic novels. Clare, a beautiful young woman with long red hair, met them at the door. Jean asked if she and Tara could just wander around. They were told, 'Of course – I'll just go and put on my make-up. Make yourselves at home.'

The house was in poor condition. It had obviously been neglected for a very long time, though here and there were signs of the beginnings of careful and tasteful renovation. The owners lived on the mainland and were restoring the house piecemeal as time and money permitted. It was, however, damp and musty and very depressing. The cellar was undeveloped, with earth floor and walls; it was like a tomb, and it was easy to understand why it was frightening. Someone had thrown coals down the stairs, and lumps were scattered about more or less at random. Jean says, 'I have been to murder scenes that were more pleasant.' Nevertheless, she found nothing specifically wrong; she could perceive no particular presence or even a hint of one. It was simply that it looked so awful.

When they went upstairs, they found that only two of the bedrooms were being used, although Clare had spoken of five or six people who shared the house with her. She had talked about her children, whom she referred to as 'my twin red-headed illegitimate daughters'. It seemed an odd way for a mother to describe her offspring, and there was no sign of them in the house – no toys, clothes or children's beds.

Finally, noticing a small black cat coiled up asleep on a dresser and responding to it as the first pleasant thing she had seen in the house, Jean went over to pet it; it was ice-cold and hard as a rock. Someone had had their pet stuffed. Jean managed not to scream and went quickly downstairs. She decided that this whole horror-movie situation must have been devised by one of her friends as a practical joke.

Clare took her into the living-room, where she met a small lady, not much larger than a dwarf, with wild blue eyes and blonde hair. She smiled and introduced herself as 'Mad Meg'. Jean thought to herself, 'They are really overdoing it', and expected people to jump out from behind the furniture and yell, 'Surprise!' This did not happen, however, so they sat down to conduct a full-scale investigation.

Tara went off to take polaroid pictures, and one of these, taken in the stair-well, showed a large, black, hairy shape; this was the part of the house where the huge rap had been heard. Jean came to the conclusion that this was no more than an image projected by Clare, who herself was intensifying the dramatic nature of the situation. There were no other indications of any presence, no cold patches, no places with notably high energy levels, and no hint of any intrusive personality or entity.

Jean told Clare that the nearby water probably explained the spectre on the stair, as running water conducts energy and, under certain atmospheric conditions, causes phantom images to appear. The hairy shape could well be a memory image left by a previous tenant or even be caused by disturbed emotions in the house. Jean added that the general decay and ugliness of the untidily industrialized neighbourhood were probably responsible for the unpleasant atmosphere in the house which had troubled her. At this, Clare burst into tears. She said that obviously Jean did not believe her story. Jean said that was not so, and reassured her, and promised to phone her in the morning.

Jean and Tara, back in their own home, discussed the situation. They agreed that the house was depressing and unpleasant, but they did not think it was truly haunted. The life-style of Clare and her friends, they felt, was probably confused and perhaps unwholesome, and this might be a contributing factor. Still, sometimes some kind of ceremony or ritual can drive away an unhappiness that feeds upon itself and grows ever stronger until the energies in the house become distorted and cause odd happenings. Clare, in any case, seemed to have such low self-esteem that a ceremony might make her feel a little more important and give her both comfort and strength. Jean telephoned Leon Reed, who is one of the most intuitive and sensitive of psychics, and asked for his help and advice. Leon agreed to join Jean and Tara in a ceremony to help Clare cope with a ghost that seemed to exist only in her mind.

On the designated night Jean, Leon and Tara met Clare and Mad Meg in the long living-room of the house. They had prepared a mini-exorcism, with special emphasis upon releasing people from the bondage of depression and unhappiness.

'Clare,' says Jean, 'was unhappy with our clothes, complaining that when she had been studying magic she wore magnificent robes. As we started the ceremony, she complained *sotto voce* about everything. We quickly finished and Leon talked to Clare, explaining what we had done and giving her a mini Tarot reading. Nothing we could say or do satisfied her. Finally I asked her why, if she had studied with a very notorious group, she had called upon us. It seemed that they had had a falling-out, and she had called on us hoping to make the group jealous. We were a great disappointment to her. After this we left.'

Later Leon said that something had appeared during the ceremony, but the situation had been so distracting that he had been unable to focus on it. They decided that the red light that moved slowly down the waterfront, about eighteen inches off the ground, was just at the level of a lantern being carried by someone searching for something, but they could arrive at no explanation. The black hairy thing on the stairs also remained unexplained.

Reflecting on the case later, Jean felt sorry that she had allowed herself to be influenced by the personalities of the people in the house to such an extent that she had been distracted from serious consideration of a subtle energy form that had really existed.

She had reason to remember the Raynor Avenue case some time later. Two Australian nurses brought her the story. They were admirably commonsensical young women, both strong and brave, and they were touring the world and stopping for a while in each place that appealed to them. It was their custom to work for a few months in each place they liked in order to earn enough money for the next leg of their journey, and Jean met them when they were working at the same hospital as her husband. They told her that in Africa they had slept in an open hut with Masai warriors and shared their breakfast of fresh milk and blood; they had stayed for two days in a deserted temple in India because of the heavy rains, their only companions being a large family of cobras. They were fearless young women.

When they arrived in Victoria, they explored the historic spots on foot. Not far from the town centre they found an old and seemingly derelict house surrounded by a fence, hedges and an overgrown garden beside an inlet of sparkling clear water. The smell of freshly cut lawns, and the sight of boats floating past, attracted them. They thought it was a perfect place to camp out, and the price was certainly right, for the lodging was free. They went back into town for a quick, cheap supper and a few more hours of tourist adventures. As twilight descended, they followed Bay Street back to Pleasant Street, laughing and saying that only pleasant things could happen to them on a street so named. When they arrived at the house by the water, it seemed even more welcoming. Cosy corners abounded and they finally chose to lay their sleeping-bags in a place by the water under the shade of some bushes. They unrolled their sleeping-bags, zipped themselves in and talked together for a while of the beauty of the night and of Victoria while sharing a bar of chocolate.

At last they both fell asleep, only to awake suddenly in terror. A threatening small figure was screaming 'Get out! Get out! How dare you!' They were out of their sleeping-bags in seconds, jumping to their feet, grabbing their belongings and stuffing things in sacks; then suddenly they realized that there was nobody there at all. No threatening figure existed. Feeling silly about their fears, they decided to slither back into the sleeping-bags and go back to sleep. As soon as the thought came into their minds, wave after wave of disapproval amounting to sheer hatred came from the house. Never, in all their adventures, had they been so frightened. The old clichés all applied: their blood ran cold and they shook with fear.

They grabbed their clothes and the bags and ran down the road to Bay Street. There they straightened their clothes, got dressed, packed their belongings once again and spent the night sitting on the bridge across the inlet. They tried to sit with their backs towards the area they had left but kept feeling that someone was sneaking up behind them, and so they sat all night staring down the inlet towards the brooding house. Once they saw a red light, like a lantern, slowly moving along the opposite shore only a little way above the ground. At this point Jean remembered Raynor Avenue.

The morning after their adventure the two nurses applied for work in a local hospital and found a small apartment.

Jean told this story to Inez O'Reilly, the owner of the house in question, who said, 'Of course, it was grandmother! She would be offended by trespass, and even more so because two young ladies certainly shouldn't be sleeping outdoors.' The house, number 2616 Pleasant Street, was Point Ellice House, a fifteen-room one-level structure that was built in 1867 for Peter O'Reilly and his wife Caroline. Peter O'Reilly was an important figure in Victorian society, having been the first Gold Commissioner of British Columbia and a close friend of Chief Justice Matthew Baillie Begbie.

The O'Reillys moved into the house in early December, and on 31 December Kathleen O'Reilly was born there. Familiarly known as 'Kit', and sometimes 'Kitty' or 'Pussy', she became one of the most glamorous ladies of Victoria, and an independent spirit. Her birth was followed by that of two boys, Arthur John, who married Mary Wyndham and Frank, who married Jessie Blackstone. John's son John Wyndham O'Reilly became the last O'Reilly to own Point Ellice House; Frank's two sons returned to the United Kingdom and remained there.

The O'Reilly world rotated around Kathleen. At twenty-five she was courted by Harry Stanhope, Lord Chesterfield's heir. His full name was Henry Athole Scudamore-Stanhope; he was twelve years older than Kathleen, and a lieutenant in the Royal Navy. Everyone expected their engagement to be announced, but Kathleen met Robert Falcon Scott, who was closer to her own age, having been born on 6 June 1868, and she fell in love with him. Unfortunately the affair was one-sided. Scott did not marry her and only a few years later, in 1900, began his explorations of the Antarctic which led to his death in 1912. Even though Scott was not for her, Kathleen realized she could not accept Stanhope's offer of marriage and felt a little guilty at having encouraged his affection, as her surviving letters reveal. They did, however, remain friends until they died, he in 1934, she ten years later, and their correspondence provides a fascinating picture of the period. Neither of them married.

At twenty-nine Kathleen visited her father's homeland, Ireland, and was presented to the Lord Lieutenant, Lord Cadogan, in Dublin Castle, which was the equivalent of being presented at Court. During the following years she travelled extensively but always returned to her birthplace. During the First World War, however, those ties were temporarily broken, for, together with her mother and her brother John, she was occupied in some form of war work in Britain, leaving Frank to look after Point Ellice House and the family lands and properties, Peter O'Reilly having died some years earlier. It is not clear exactly what happened, but when Caroline, Kathleen and John returned at the end of the war, they discovered that the family fortune had disappeared. Land, houses and buildings in central Victoria had all been sold and there was little money in the bank. Unable to maintain their position in society, Kathleen and Caroline withdrew from public life.

Kathleen kept a hat, purse and gloves on a table near the front door. When company approached, she would put on her hat and gloves, meet her friends at the gate and say, 'I was just going to the Empress [Hotel] for tea. Won't you please join me?' None of their friends was ever invited to the house.

After the death of Caroline, Kathleen lived on in the house with a female relative. There were no more balls or teas or jaunts to Europe, no more admirers, only a sequence of dreary days, one the same as another. This period of dreariness, hopelessness and unhappiness may have been the incubation period for later hauntings. In 1945 Kathleen died in the house in which she was born.

Mary O'Reilly, Kathleen's sister-in-law, lived in the house until 1964. Before she died, plans had been made for the house to be torn down and the land sold for industrial development. This was not to happen. In 1965 her son John met and married Inez, who once said that it was partly her immediate love of the house when she first entered it that led her to marry him.

Not long after John and Inez had made 2616 Pleasant Street their home, Inez had a strange experience.

'One day,' she said, 'we came back from a trip. I was left alone in the drawing-room and suddenly felt that I was alone in a complete vacuum. I felt arms around me, and I knew that the arms were those of Grandmother O'Reilly (Caroline), and a tremendous desire to save the house from destruction came over me.'

By practising thrift and using a great deal of elbow-grease, John and Inez rescued the house which had been lived in by the same family for over a hundred years and which was full of the accumulations of those years. Renewing the house and returning it to its original splendour were both a trial and a joy. Boxes of household stuff were found in the garden among the bushes. It seems that whenever Caroline got tired of a set of dinnerware, or a vase or two, she would put the discarded material in the garden. Broken crockery and even fragments split off the mouldings or the mantelpiece would be similarly treated, and when these were brought back in the house, they were found to fit perfectly into place. It appears that absolutely nothing was allowed to leave the property, whether broken or not. John and Inez tried to keep all the family treasures, and they consulted old photographs to discover the original disposition of the pictures and furniture. The cost was appalling, but they persevered.

At one point, when a new roof was needed, Inez sent a samovar off to an auction in Toronto. It was so impressive a piece that a photograph of it was used as the cover picture of the catalogue. People went to the preview just to see it, and there was hardly a moment when it was not surrounded by a small group of admirers. When the auction occurred, however, not one single bid was made on the samovar. It was returned to Victoria, and the money that was needed was found elsewhere. Inez said, 'Of course! Grandmother didn't want it sold. I should have known that she would arrange for the money to reach us.'

Finally ready for public showing, Point Ellice House was opened as a privately owned living museum in 1967. One of the first visitors was an elderly lady with her 4-year-old granddaughter. Once inside the door, the child threw a hysterical fit. The grandmother took her outside and scolded Inez, saying, 'You should warn people that the house is haunted. We should sue you. It's very dangerous.' Inez had a sign painted reading, 'This House Is Haunted', but members of local civic groups complained that the sign was unseemly. Inez therefore had the sign repainted to read, 'This House is haunted by the ghosts of the past,' and hoped that in this way she could satisfy everyone.

Several ladies dressed in Victorian costume acted as hostesses and guides. One day, when Jean was visiting, Inez was the only person on duty. As they talked, an American couple arrived. Inez said, 'Please look around. I'll be with you in a moment,' but as she and Jean continued to talk of an upcoming CBC Special about the house, they realized that the couple were leaving.

Inez said, 'Please. Let me give you a tour of the house.'

They said politely, 'No, thank you. The young lady showed us around and explained everything.'

Inez said, 'There's no one here but me!' and they said, 'Oh yes, she was dressed in a blue dress.'

Taking them to Kathleen's room, Inez pointed to a blue dress hanging on the wall, and they agreed that this was what their guide had been wearing.

On another occasion two young men claimed that they had seen Kathleen leaning on the gate as they arrived and that she had followed them down the street when they left. One time a Japanese television crew arrived to photograph the house for a

TV programme called *Strange World*. Jean described for them how she had taken a group of members of the Vancouver Island Society for Psychical Research on a tour of the house.

'We found,' said Jean, 'a cold spot about two feet by two feet where the temperature was twelve degrees colder than the rest of the room. A medium in the visiting group said several ghosts were present: Grandmother, who didn't really approve of the museum but who was willing to help just to keep the house in the family, and two men and one woman who wanted the house to be totally destroyed.'

Jean also told them of seeing twenty people warming their hands and saying how great the fire felt, even though the fire in the big stove had been extinguished forty years earlier. Anne Dunae, the mother of the young man who had seen the April Ghost on Oak Bay Golf Course, sitting on a courting bench in the garden saw a handsome young man in old-fashioned dress. As the group were leaving, they asked Jean's name, so that they could be sure to spell it correctly. A young man then asked for the names of the other two young ladies, who were wearing period costumes. There were no such ladies.

'One Hallowe'en at midnight CFAX Radio took us to the house,' Jean says. 'It was wet and dreary and, while nothing exciting happened, one polaroid picture showed the outline of the head and shoulders of a woman who did not exist. And the announcer's voice cracked on several occasions when the house made creaking noises. Then I realized that on the many other times I had visited the house it had never made any of the usual house-settling noises.'

As the years passed, it became clear that even Grandmother Caroline would be unable to keep the house in the family. The costly restoration had caused an unreasonable increase in house taxes. Point Ellice House was sold to the Provincial Government in 1974 for $455,000. From that time until the present day work has continued on the house and its contents. The old kitchen middens have been explored, and broken china has been discovered and reassembled. New preservation techniques are being used, and the enormous quantity of material is still being catalogued.

When we decided to write this book, Jean felt she should go back to Point Ellice House for a visit, arriving – typically – on a day when the house was closed to the public. She walked through the gardens, and the opium poppies reminded her of the Victorian heritage of Oriental gardeners.

'The grounds were lovely,' she says, 'but there was still a strange, timeless feeling. An invisible company shared the gardens with me that afternoon. Later in the week Tara and I went back again. We were let in by a delightful curator. The house was lovely but still in transition; even after fifteen years there is still much work to be done. After a pleasant tour, we told of the nurses' adventure and began to talk of the ghosts. Someone still taps people on the shoulder and whispers in their ears, but not quite distinctly enough to be understood, we were told, and one cleaner refuses to go into Kathleen's room.'

Jean always suggests that ghosts should be set free. She does not think it healthy to live with presences of the dead. In this case, however, she feels that the enterprising ghost of Grandmother Caroline still protects and preserves the house and that Kathleen, who during her life could never bring herself to leave her home, deserves to decide for herself how long she needs to stay there.

Point Ellice House itself is as pleasant as any house on a street named Pleasant should be, but the atmosphere in the garden is changeable. Jean and Tara discovered on a recent visit that in the evening, as the shadows lengthen and the water becomes a deep shade of lavender, the atmosphere becomes heavy and threatening, quite unlike that of the house animated by the wholesome female energies of Caroline and Kathleen. As they left the grounds, they stopped to read the inscription on a horse-trough covered in ivy that stands by the parking-lot. The inscription read 'Bridge End', and they understood the reason for their disquietude.

There was indeed a bridge over the water at this place. It was called Point Ellice Bridge, and in 1896 it was the scene of one of the worst street-car (tram) disasters in North American history. The story is told by Terry Reksten in her book about Victoria, *More English than the English*, and her account runs as follows:

> The Queen's Birthday celebrations in 1896 promised to be … spectacular. In addition to the Gorge regatta, the climax of the four day holiday was to be a military tattoo and a sham battle, staged at Macauley Point on Tuesday, May 26.
>
> At about twenty minutes to two that Tuesday afternoon, Car 6, one of the company's older, smaller, lighter cars left town for the Point Ellice Bridge followed by Car 16, newer, larger and carrying more than 140 passengers. As they neared the bridge, Car 16 slowed to allow the first car to reach the end of the span and a woman tourist from Seattle took advantage of the lull to ask the conductor to open her window, an insignificant act that probably saved her life.
>
> Once the first car had gained the opposite bank, Car 16 rolled forward. After it had travelled thirty or forty feet, there was an odd cracking sound and Car 16 dropped a foot and a half. It continued to move forward for a second or two and then the air was split by a second loud crack and the street car and the collapsing center span of the bridge plunged down into the water below.
>
> Pleasure boaters, who had been spending a lazy afternoon idling along the Gorge, were jolted into action and paddled furiously for the submerged car while water-side residents scrambled down the bank to the nearest boathouse. Soon a small armada had converged below the bridge's broken span. Exhibiting heroism, or at least presence of mind, the Tyrwhitt-Drake girls managed to pull seven choking people from the water. As the *Colonist* would note approvingly, 'class distinctions were forgotten.'
>
> Too soon only lifeless bodies were being hauled out of the water to be laid side-by-side on well-groomed lawns. Women from Gorge-side houses tore curtains from their windows to serve as blankets and shrouds and rushed to and fro with brandy, trying to comfort survivors who stumbled about among the corpses looking for the child,

the husband or wife, the brother or sister or friend who had been beside them when the bridge collapsed.

The final death count was appalling. Fifty-five men, women and children were dead – crushed by the falling bridge timbers or trapped in the streetcar and drowned. Before Victorians fully appreciated the enormity of the disaster, or began to ask awkward questions about its cause, odd stories, the quirks of fate that had saved some and doomed others, began to emerge.

Three horse drawn carriages had been setting out across the bridge at the same time as Car 16. Two had proceeded and had been thrown into the water. Both drivers survived, but the horses trapped in their harnesses had drowned. The third driver had been spared the ordeal when his horse, suddenly and for no apparent reason, reared in its traces and wheeled about carrying him to safety.

'The most extraordinary things happened,' a survivor remembered. 'People inside were shot out – nobody knows how – of broken windows.'

'My friend ... the beam hit him on the back of the head and took his head off nearly. Oh, there was a lot of young girls in the front ... when the bridge came down with all the iron work on top, these girls were caught in there, and they had to take blowtorches the next day and cut the wires out to get those two girls out of that mixture. Terrible thing!' The girls, he shuddered, had only been a few feet from him.

There are many other stories of what happened on that terrible day. It is said that the butler of one house, when approached for sheets to cover the bodies laid out on the bank in front of the house, refused to help and firmly closed the door in the faces of the applicants. The intensity of the emotions of shock and grief must have affected the whole area around, and it seems that the red light that moves along the bank of the gorge on the side opposite Point Ellice House may well be the spectral lantern of someone still searching for a lost loved-one.

The new bridge over the inlet is commonly known as the Bay Street Bridge, but in fact the old name is still the correct one. 'Point Ellice Bridge' the sign says firmly, and not far away is another sign pointing to Point Ellice House, the house that is haunted by ghosts of the past.

8

Dancing and Dining with Ghosts

I was a little surprised when the professor of military history asked me if I knew anything about ghosts. I said, rather cautiously, that I knew a few things. We were sitting over pre-prandial drinks at lunchtime in the Faculty Club. He said, 'Well, this friend of mine asked me if I knew anyone at the university who was an expert, and I thought of you.' He told me that his friend had been having problems, noises, an apparition or two and so forth, and that his wife was getting depressed. I got the name and address from him and phoned the house and made an appointment.

In actual fact I looked over the house before the arranged date. I was in that vicinity with my daughter Brigid and her friend Lawrence, so I asked them to drive me past the house. When we reached it, on an impulse I asked them to park. It was set on the side of a low hill, and the garden in front of it was raised from the ground by a stone wall; there were no flowers, only grass. The whole place had an uneasy look to it. As I looked, I saw a face at an upper window, and so I told Brigid and Lawrence to wait, and I went up and rang the bell. The daughter of the house answered the door. Fortunately she knew who I was and why I wanted to look around, and so I pottered about a bit. The house certainly felt cheerless, and there were several young, lively Dobermann Pinschers locked away in the kitchen, separated from me by a half-door, for which I was grateful. Dobermann Pinschers make me nervous, much more nervous than ghosts.

I didn't come to any definite conclusions, but when I returned to the car, both Lawrence and Brigid said the house really disturbed them. It was quite a new house, and it looked as if the whole hillside had been raped in order to create the subdivision to which it belonged. On the opposite side of the road from the house there was a stream, and no houses were built there.

I phoned Jean, and we went out to the house together one evening. Jean says that to her the house seemed 'raw or new' at first glance. As we walked up the drive alongside the raised garden, we passed a van filled with wildly snarling Dobermann Pinschers. It didn't do much for my morale, but Jean did not seem perturbed. The couple, whom I will call Barber, were waiting in the living-room, together with their teenaged son.

As usual, the phenomena had begun with deep depression. Mrs Barber had felt below par for a long time, and then one day, on emerging from the downstairs bathroom, she had seen a strange man standing watching her. For a second she believed he was real, but then he disappeared. One afternoon, as she was vacuuming the lower hall, she saw an animal run across the top of the stairs. The dogs paid it no attention, but after that they would not go upstairs. The animal she saw moved too quickly for her to be precise about it, but she said it was not a dog, but a sort of mixture. The family had the custom of leaving the incoming mail on top of the fridge in the utility room at the back of the house on the ground floor, and quite often a letter left there to be picked up by a family member would have disappeared before it could be collected.

The basement was most unpleasant. It was divided into two sections. The inner section was separated from the rest by a wire barrier; it contained two large kennels decorated with many award ribbons from dog shows. The Barbers' hobby was breeding Dobermanns. The other part was bright and clean, but it was definitely unpleasant. There were some paint marks on one or two of the walls.

Upstairs, one bedroom was very unhappy. It belonged to the daughter whom I had met, and she had told me that she found the room depressing. Jean says, 'I could feel a young child-like woman crying.'

A small door on the same level and just near the top of the stairs led to a storage area underneath the eaves. I felt immediately that there was something in there, and Jean concurred. It was, she was sure, the living-quarters of the creature Mrs Barber had seen; it was, she told me, an elemental. I agreed and we stood there meditating for a few moments. I felt that it was a spirit entity that had been trapped when the land had been cleared and the subdivision built. Jean said that this explained the theft of the mail. Elementals, being pure energy, often behave mischievously and cause things to be mislaid and even permanently lost. We decided that we should take this creature away with us and come back later to deal with the rest of the house.

Jean went downstairs and asked for a brown paper bag. We opened the door to the storage space and laid the bag inside, open, so that the elemental could crawl into it in the way in which cats so often do. We stood there and talked to the creature. I saw it as a long black creature rather like a ferret but with smooth skin not unlike that of the Dobermanns. Jean saw the same image, but in her perception it had a face not wholly unlike that of a human being. I told it firmly but kindly that it should get into the bag and we would take it away with us and put it in a place it would enjoy. Jean also spoke to it, but a little more authoritatively. Later she remarked that we had been behaving like the good cop/bad cop combination in crime fiction.

We went downstairs and described what we wished to do, leaving the elemental to its own devices. We said we would take it away with us. This would relieve the tension on the second floor and also stop the meddling with the mail. We said that the children would feel the emptiness and be disturbed, but that this feeling would soon go. There might, however, be some emotional outbursts over a short period. I also suggested that apples should be placed in the storage area, thus replacing energy that had been acting negatively with energies of ripening and a positive feeling, and following the principle that when one source of energy is removed, another must be set in its place. We arranged to return at noon the following day to complete the job, and Mr Barber agreed to let us in the house and then leave us to it for an hour or so. He also promised to have the Dobermanns locked safely away in the van.

Jean went upstairs and got the paper bag and brought it down to the living-room before we made our farewells. Mrs Barber said the animal she had seen was too large to fit into that bag, and we had to explain that it could take on any size or shape it wished. I was myself amused and a bit surprised that Mrs Barber accepted with such simplicity that the creature would enter the bag. I am sure I would have been much more sceptical. Indeed, I found the whole situation bizarre and even ludicrous.

Nevertheless, the elemental was in the bag. We could feel the restless energy of it as we put the bag in the car and tried to decide where to let the creature free. I made a number of suggestions, proposing the gardens of people whom I disliked or distrusted and who, I felt, could benefit from a little disturbance, but I did not mean my suggestions to be taken seriously. Still, we both giggled about it a little, and finally we settled on the native plant park in Oak Bay, a small wild area into which few people ever ventured and where the plants and trees were sure never to be disturbed by human activity. Jean took the bag from the car, speaking comfortingly to its quiet inhabitant, and opened it in a patch of St John's wort by an old gnarled oak tree. We left the creature there, assured that it would make its home in that place.

A few days later we went back to the house at noon, as arranged, with Tara as a third member of the group with her camera. The van was in the driveway full of leaping and noisy dogs. They were not, however, as noisy as previously, and Mr Barber had told us that they had grown a good deal more quiet since the removal of the elemental. Upstairs the house felt somewhat more pleasant but was still uneasy. The storage space did not contain apples but gaily wrapped Christmas gifts. This, I reckoned, would do just as well as apples, or even better, for each gift carried with it an energy of blessing and even love.

We went down to the basement. At first I had assumed that the Dobermann Pinschers' area might be a trouble spot, but in fact it felt just fine. The rest of the basement, however, had an energy that was somehow destructive and unhealthy. Jean remembered that earlier the Barbers had told us that when they bought the house they had found a lot of scrawls and paint marks in the basement where, it seems, some young people had been having meetings or partying. When Mrs Barber told us this, she averted her eyes from the pentagrams that both Jean and I were wearing, so Jean suspected that some of the signs might have been magical and that perhaps the young people had been meddling in the occult, or pretending to meddle in it. This made sense. The period in question was one during which many people were attracted to the melodramatic magic-ridden adventures of 'Dungeons and Dragons'. Nevertheless, as I wandered around, I felt something quite different.

The concrete wall facing the front of the house caught my attention. There was still a smear or two of paint on it, red paint. I felt there was energy remaining there. I sprinkled some salt on the little ledge where the foundation concrete gave way to the walls of the house proper, and I stood there and breathed in the atmosphere. I sensed something almost immediately. It was dancing. It was not modern dancing, however; it was the kind of dance that you will see at American Indian dance festivals. But I did not think these youths – they were youths, I was sure – were true Indians. They were experimenting, I felt, and they were emotionally disturbed. They might have been Indian, or they might have been others pretending to be Indian, but their energies were not securely based in real beliefs. I felt I had to communicate with these presences, and I began myself to do the half-shuffle half-dance that I had seen so many times and that, somehow, came naturally to me. I danced quite a short time, and mostly without moving very much. You could call it, I suppose, dancing on the spot. Then, suddenly, I knew I had their attention, and I said mentally, quite without thinking, 'I can dance a damn sight better than you. Get out!' and I was, for a second, an authority figure to them. I said to Tara, perhaps even a little sharply, 'Open the door.' She opened it, and I knew that they had gone.

Jean said, 'The basement's better now. In fact, it's just fine', and Tara agreed. We stayed there a while, adding positive energy with blessings to replace the energies that had left, and, we felt, the job was done.

We warned the Barbers that in the next twenty-four hours they could expect a disturbance or two, and they said they understood. (People often say that and are then surprised and upset when something happens.) Mrs Barber bore the brunt of it. She heard her son come into the house and call out to her. She responded, but there was nobody there. As he had left the house only twenty minutes before, she became very upset and had thoughts of his having been killed by a car accident or something of that kind. Later, in her bedroom, which was just over the once unpleasant part of the basement, such a wave of depression came over her that she lay on the bed weeping.

Mr Barber phoned me that evening. I said he should not worry. In fact, the new disturbances were a sign that the job had been done satisfactorily. A few days later he rang again. He was effusive in his thanks. He said his wife was behaving like a new woman. She was lively and vital again, as she had never been since they moved into the house. He said he wanted to tell me this personally and rang off. A little later that same night Mrs Barber rang up. She said she felt I ought to know that her husband was no longer as depressed as he had been ever since they moved into the house, that he was a new man and seemed younger. I chuckled happily.

There was, however, one problem remaining: that of the spectre. I told Mr Barber that if he was troubled by the remembrance of this he could deal with the problem fairly easily. The stream on the opposite side of the road was clearly fed by water running down under the hill; the house was therefore built over running water. I said that, if he would get three iron stakes, I would show him where to plant them in his back yard so that they would divert the electro-magnetic field. He said he would do that, but I did not hear from him again. I checked on him, though, by way of our mutual friend, the professor of military history, who told me that there had been no more trouble.

Rituals and ceremonies, even amateurish ones like those performed in the Barbers' house, frequently leave an energy field behind them, as do performances of plays in which people express intense emotion. Consequently both actors and theatres are somewhat vulnerable to haunting. Indeed, it is well known that a great many actors are so much aware of the psychic dimension of their profession that they carry talismans, wear the same garment for all their roles and have many superstitions. Theatres are, of course, frequently haunted. In Victoria three of the theatres possess ghosts.

The McPherson Theatre is perhaps the most interesting case. A friend of ours was working as a nightwatchman there in recent months, and he came across two disturbances. Once, while on the stage, he looked across at the taut ropes that run from the stage up to the flies and that are firmly fixed both top and bottom, and just one of the group of them was moving, and it was moving rapidly and strongly, as if it were animated by an enormous energy. Just at that point he heard footsteps on the fly gallery above, and yet he was alone in the theatre. He avoided that part of the stage thereafter and, on asking around, learned that a stage hand had suffered an accident in that place.

On another occasion the phenomenon was much more difficult to explain. It was 2.30 in the morning when, quite suddenly, he heard loud voices in the green room. It sounded like a party. Again he was alone in the theatre, which was securely locked against intruders, and intruders would, in any case, be unlikely to throw a noisy party.

But why would there be ghosts in a theatre at 2.30 in the morning? The cast and the stage hands have always left before that hour. Jean came to the conclusion that the answer is probably: gambling. What more private and protected space than an empty theatre in the small wee hours? Thinking this over, she remembered one of the local ghosts. He was called 'the Frenchman'.

It is said that one of the sons of the wealthy and influential Dunsmuir family was known to be a considerable gambler. The local devotees of this pastime knew he was also something of a sucker, and so they would lure him into games and relieve him of his money. It seems that one night, in 1892, somewhere in the vicinity of the theatre, he was playing poker with two of his close friends when an argument broke out. A young Frenchman, a visitor to Victoria, was fatally shot. The company were horrified and foresaw not only trouble with the police but also enormous scandal. Two of young Dunsmuir's friends picked up the body and, carrying it between them as if he were drunk, took him out of the building and to the corner of Government and Fisgard Streets, and sat him down, propping him up against a tree, where he was found the next morning. The crime was never solved, but local gossip had no doubt about what had occurred.

The ghost of the Frenchman is seen on October mornings at nine or 9.30, sitting on the street corner, wearing a long beige coat like a modern raincoat. His hair and beard are brown, and his cheeks are rosy. Of course, soon after he has been seen, he disappears. It is pure speculation that the fatal gambling game took place in the theatre, but the Frenchman is the only gambler ghost that has come to our attention, so it may be that we have found a solution.

The MacPherson Theatre is not alone in being haunted. The Langham Court Theatre boasts a ghost which has been called 'the Lady in the Loft', and there is a most unpleasant presence in the boiler-room of the Royal Theatre and in one of the theatre boxes. These presences have so far remained unexplained.

Actors are, as I have said, particularly vulnerable to psychic disturbances, perhaps because it is their business to take on alien personalities while following their profession. I do not think it is coincidence that the lady living in Heather Street was an actress. Indeed, at this time she had a way of changing her appearance, her hair-style, her mode of dress and even to some extent her gestures so frequently that, although I knew her well, it sometimes took me several seconds to recognize her.

The house in which she lived was, she told me, depressed. One room in particular was most depressing and remained so however often she and the man of the house redecorated it. I knew the house well, and agreed with her. I also thought that the house might have something to do with the man's occasional bouts of melancholia, two of which had landed him in hospital after taking an overdose of pills. I therefore agreed to do something about the house and called Jean.

In preparation for an exorcism Jean asked Tara to type out the ceremony. Tara was in the middle of typing when Jean, unable to decide what colour candles should be used, interrupted her in her work and asked her advice. Tara, cross at being interrupted, snapped, 'Purple and orange!' Tara was often tense while typing but seemed to be more tense and upset than usual, so Jean went away and left her to it. However, when they both arrived at Heather Street, Jean says, 'The door opened and we saw the staircase, and it had bannister spindles painted alternately purple and orange, all the way up to the landing at the top.'

'Brenda' was a petite woman with brown hair and a rather sharp-chinned, piquant face, but when Jean saw her for the first time, she perceived her as 'a large lady tall and sturdy with short dark red hair. She was wearing 1920ish evening pyjamas, had a very dramatic voice, and moved her hands in an exaggerated manner. She showed us over the house and, pointing to a couch under the window, said, "He tried to commit suicide three times on that couch. You have no idea how hard it is to get out the bloodstains." This remark was completely out of step with what I had been told about the house. I had been assured, by Robin, that no violence had ever taken place there and that the problems had been mainly emotional. I did not stop and ask her about the suicide attempts or the blood as I did not wish to break the chain of the mood she was feeling, but I felt that the comment sounded like something out of a very bad play.'

Before we began our work we had to wait for the man of the house and his Japanese house-guest to leave for a party. The guest had very little English, and nobody could work out how to tell him what was going on. Unhappily he was tired after his journey, for he had only just arrived in Victoria and could not understand why he was being bustled off to a party while Sylvia and I, who were also friends of his, were staying behind. Eventually he was manoeuvred out of the door, baffled but amenable, and we began the process of sealing the house with sticks of incense.

Sylvia and Tara circled the inside of the house in one direction, and I accompanied Brenda. Several times she told me she could not go on, that she felt something was holding her back. It was quite a tussle to get her past the back door which led to the garden, for example, and I had to urge her to go on and even help her wave the smoking stick of incense over the doorway. Eventually, however, the sealing was accomplished, and we began the ceremony in the living-room, not by the front door as usual, for Jean had decided that in this case we needed to place ourselves within a formal circle. I did not at the time understand why.

Jean remembers that, 'In the middle part of the exorcism, when we began to expel the spirits, Brenda started to breathe very heavily and then to snarl and spit like an angry cat. Quickly and silently Robin took Sylvia's and Tara's hands and joined them around Brenda, enclosing her in a tight circle. She lurched from side to side, trying to break their hold, screaming to be let go. It took all of their strength to hold her.'

My recollection is the same as Jean's, except that I am not sure who exactly initiated the imprisoning circle of arms. I rather think Tara and I thought of it at the same time. It was, however, astonishing just how strong Brenda had become. I am a big man, and Sylvia and Tara are both strong women, but we were staggering and straining to keep this petite person under control. Jean continued with the banishing ritual as we struggled. She maintains that the struggle lasted for more than twenty minutes. I do not think it lasted quite that long, but we were certainly growing exhausted before Brenda began to weaken and to sob and beg us to please let her go out of the circle.

Jean recalls that, 'Robin told Sylvia and Tara to hang on and under no circumstances to let her go. Picking up the protection oil, I managed to rub some on Brenda's forehead. She screamed when it touched her skin, but slowly became quiet, and the sobbing turned first to hiccups and then to agonizing dry-retching, as if she were vomiting up something.'

As soon as I heard and felt her retching, I knew that the task was complete. She sagged in exhaustion against Sylvia, leaning her head on her shoulder, and I made comforting noises, telling her she was all right, that she was a good girl, that there was nothing to worry about now, and so forth, and we all three held her in a comforting fashion. Slowly we released her, and Jean says, 'A tiny little lady with dark hair and a tear-streaked face smiled up at us. The red-haired woman I had seen had been not Brenda herself but a spiritual obsession that had possessed her to the point of changing her appearance.'

She was still tearful when we led her out of the circle and sat her down on the couch to recover, but in a very short time she was not only calm but happy. She felt both relief and gladness, she told us, but she had no recollection at all of what had happened in the circle. Later she discovered that she had lost five pounds in weight.

We waited for the candles to burn out, and when they had done so and it was time for the house to be blessed, Brenda asked if she could do that part herself. Quietly she took each article from the altar to an appropriate place and pronounced blessings. When she picked up the bread, she walked to her man's writing-desk and placed it on his blotter, because she wanted him to become prosperous. 'I want him to have a lot of bread,' she said, laughing.

'Never have I seen such a change,' Jean says, 'and she asked if she could borrow Tara's silver dragon pendant to use as a talisman the next morning when she finished the ceremony by burying the bread in the garden and pouring the water, wine and salt over the place.'

Several times during the evening there had been phone calls from our Japanese friend, positively pleading to be allowed to come home, on each occasion sounding more and more weary and less and less sober. When at last we were able to phone him, we discovered that he was the very last guest remaining at the party and felt more than a little guilty. He did return in relatively good order, however, and the following morning, when the situation was explained to him, he understood perfectly.

Brenda performed the burial in the garden satisfactorily, using a spot underneath an apple tree. Several hours later she phoned Tara in a panic. The dragon pendant was gone. Tara comforted her and went over to help her look for it. Hours later, after an exhaustive search, they went outside for a breath of fresh air. Something sparkling caught their eye. They found the dragon swinging to and fro on its silver chain from a branch of the apple tree.

We are still unsure about the exact nature of the spirit which possessed Brenda. At first we thought that the entity inhabiting the house had simply moved into her as a way of avoiding exorcism. Then we wondered if this strong woman entity had been created as a consequence of some of the parts Brenda had played as an actress, and that it had been so vividly conjured up in performance that it had remained.

Actors do create thought forms and have been known unintentionally to conjure up the dead. I was once called to the phone by Marilyn Bowering, whose play about Marilyn Monroe was being performed at the Open Space Theatre in Victoria. She tells the story:

'My play about Marilyn Monroe, *Anyone Can See I Love You*, opened in Victoria in January of 1988. The action of the play takes place in a rehearsal space that gradually – as the three musicians (who also portray Monroe's three husbands) oversee a Marilyn who is reliving and reviewing her life – becomes her tomb. Much of the play is a re-creation of Marilyn Monroe's voice, and this combined with the remarkable performance of Lenore Zann, who looked, breathed, spoke and sang like Marilyn, made for a powerful and almost eerie production. On opening night there was a brief, sudden and unpredicted storm that blew open the doors of the theatre. People said, jokingly, that it was Marilyn Monroe trying to get in.

'On the Wednesday night, about a week into the run, I had a deeply disturbing "dream". I dreamed first that there was a very small child, a blonde little girl about three years old, sleeping, and that this child was cold on her arm and her shoulder. I knew, in the dream, that the child was cold because the spirit of Marilyn Monroe was trying to enter her. Then I became the object of the spirit's attentions and felt extremely cold on my arm and shoulder. The spirit in the dream was not exactly visible, although I would say that it took up space, but its nature – unhappy, restless, fragmented – and its identity were beyond question.

'I didn't like this dream, nor the feeling it brought, and so I tried very hard to wake up. When I awoke, I checked, because my arm was still extremely cold, to see if it was lying outside the covers: however, I was completely and snugly covered from neck to feet. The cold then moved along my arm and shoulder and up onto my face. I disliked this intensely and realized that I needed to be, as it were, at the top of my consciousness to combat it. As I struggled to become fully alert, there was a great and suffocating weight on my chest so that I could scarcely breathe. After what felt like a very long time, and in no doubt that I was being threatened, I managed to rid myself of this aggressive and unpleasant sensation.

'It was several hours before I was able to get back to sleep.

'The feeling of disturbance persisted throughout the next day. Worried by this, I telephoned Lenore Zann to ask her about the previous evening's performance. I did not tell her about my experience. After several minutes of conversation she told me that the musicians had said to her the night before that when she came through the archway (in the play it is a symbolic entrance into death) at the end, it was as if a ghost had appeared.

'Feeling rather out of my depth, and concerned for the actors in the play, I telephoned Robin to ask his advice. And so I quartered an onion and placed it in the four corners of the bedroom, sprinkled salt around the bed (and later on told Lenore Zann to put salt in her shoes) and wrote on a paper which I placed in a spell-box, "I send you, spirits, to light and rest."

'Apparently they or she paid attention. The onion dried up in the normal manner, and the ghost did not bother me again.'

The spectre of Marilyn Monroe was not conjured up wholly by Marilyn Bowering's words, or by the performance of the actress. It was also created by the audience, for in any place where many people gather together and allow their emotional lives some freedom, this kind of haunting often occurs.

Restaurants, like theatres, are not infrequently the location of hauntings, though it does not seem that the ghosts have anything to do with the food. It may be possible that a place where people congregate and relax can create, if not a vortex, at least a place receptive to psychic phenomena. Possibly the excitement and the 'vibrations' of a crowd of people may rouse images from the past.

Several Victoria restaurants have been haunted. One particularly interesting and, indeed, entertaining haunting took place in Bastion Square. Number 31 Bastion Square is now the Board of Trade Building, but in the 1970s it housed, in its basement, a restaurant called the Barbary Banjo. Jean went there one day for lunch with her friends Betty and Cece. Betty had been there several times in the evening for dinner and a sing-along. The decor and atmosphere were Gay Nineties, and the music was also evocative of that period. Such songs as 'A Bird in a Gilded Cage' and 'The Man on the Flying Trapeze' were featured. The three friends decided to avoid talking about haunted houses or psychic experiences or anything of that kind, but after they had ordered lunch Jean had an odd experience.

'Everything,' she says, 'went just a little out of focus. Another scene was superimposed upon that of the people having lunch around us. Large men dressed in long white or beige coats of what looked like canvas, with longish hair, beards and bowler-type hats were pushing crates around and carrying barrels on their shoulders. Three men dressed in white shirts and ties with sleeve garters pushed a white piano into the room.

I thought, "How unusual to have a white piano in a warehouse" and then I realized that they were the waiters moving the Barbary Banjo's piano. For a few moments both scenes were equally vivid.

'Suddenly the atmosphere changed. A man wearing a black jacket jumped up on a crate and began an impassioned speech to the men gathered around him and listening intently. It was obviously an emotionally charged situation. I realized that I could not hear any sounds, however, and I looked at my lunch companions, and it was clear that I was the only one who could see this strange scene. Later I was told that this square had housed a police station, and in the prison next door to it people had been tried and executed and then buried in the square. The bodies were dug up and transferred to Ross Bay Cemetery in the 1930s.'

After some time the Barbary Banjo changed hands and became the Little Denmark Restaurant, and Mario, who had been a member of the group seance in the house on the hill, told Jean that he knew the manager, who had told him of his experiences in the place.

After lunch the manager always had a nap in his office, and every day regularly at 3.15 the electric eye in the main doorway would buzz, as if someone were there, but nobody ever was. Each morning dishes would be found broken and tables disturbed. Taps would be running and lights, which had been carefully turned off the previous night, would be found burning brightly. One night, as a joke, a glass of gin was left on the piano. The next morning everything was found in perfect order, but the glass of gin was empty. Thereafter it became the regular custom to leave a glass of gin for whoever or whatever enjoyed it in the night. The staff joked that they had either an alcoholic ghost or a mighty happy mouse. One night when the waiter forgot to put out the glass of gin, the restaurant was once again found disturbed in the morning, with lights on, taps running and dishes piled in heaps on the floor.

As Jean was not asked to do anything about the ghost, she did not attempt any kind of exorcism. One cannot intrude on such situations without being asked, and people who have haunted houses often feel that even enquiries are an invasion of their privacy. However, we always say a small blessing on these displaced persons when we encounter them, and bless the place which is being disturbed. If we had investigated the restaurant, the two most obvious clues were the piano, since it was involved both in the luncheon experience and in the later one of the gin-drinker. Was an entertainer once incarcerated in the gaol, and had his restless spirit been attracted by the party atmosphere and the music with which he might have been familiar, or even performed in his own time?

Number 31 Bastion Square now houses stacks of records and books, and it is perhaps to be hoped that the workers there do not play the radio very often, especially not those stations that feature music of earlier times.

The Barbary Banjo's ghosts at least did not upset the customers or send them away, for it was a popular eating-place. This was not so with another restaurant, which I will call the Fox & Grapes, because that was never its name and it is still a restaurant.

I was telephoned one day by the proprietor, who told us he was having problems and they just might be caused by some kind of ghost. Sylvia and Alison and I went out to lunch there and took Jean along with us. The dining-room was almost empty; there was only one other table occupied. The proprietor told us that he simply could not get customers, and that over and over again people would walk up the path to his front door and then turn around and go away again. This he could not understand, for not only was the bill of fare first-class but there was no alternative restaurant nearby for them to have lunch. Moreover, he could not keep kitchen help. One man had recently left abruptly without an explanation; another had refused to work in the place, although he was unemployed at the time. He asked us if we could help him.

We looked around the place. It was not unpleasant but somehow dispirited, and there was an ugly hunting trophy over the front door. I told him to take it away. It was not helping the atmosphere at all and even had a threatening quality.

The building, we learned, had originally been a home for a retired couple. During the clearing of the ground a workman engaged in dynamiting a tree stump had died from the explosion. Before the house had been completed, the husband died and his widow opened the house as a tea-room. The next owner expanded the business and turned the place into a restaurant. Our troubled acquaintance was now doing his best to create a better-class restaurant with a sophisticated menu and a good wine list.

We felt that the two deaths and the widow's grief probably accounted for the depressed atmosphere, and we asked the proprietor on which night of the week the restaurant was closed. He said Tuesday, and we told him that we could come around the following Tuesday and deal with the problem. Jean, Alison and I had all received a strong feeling that the path up to the front door demanded a blessing, if not an actual exorcism, and that the land upon which the building stood had to be cleansed. We were all prepared to do our work and were very sorry for the proprietor, who seemed a pleasant man.

A few days later the restaurant-owner phoned and told Sylvia that he no longer wished us to help. He said he had spoken to the minister of his local church and had been told firmly that he must have nothing to do with 'those people'. Sylvia asked him if the minister would then perform a Christian exorcism. He said he would not. He had indeed refused to do so. This upset us all a good deal, not so much because a Christian minister had warned him against us, for that was perfectly intelligible. Christian authorities are not usually sympathetic to witches. We were, however, angry that this minister had himself refused to help.

Some weeks later we heard the news. Our restaurateur had suffered a serious breakdown and was in the mental hospital, and he had lost his restaurant.

I do not know whether or not the present restaurant on the site is facing problems; I hope not. It may be that our sometime friend was himself a vulnerable person and attracted spiritual disturbance. This is often the case. Some people do attract psychic phenomena, and others are either oblivious to them or actually repel them. There is no yardstick by which one can measure a person's vulnerability or receptiveness, and we have no satisfactory explanations of why this should be so. All we can say is that it seems that not only are theatres and restaurants particularly prone to psychic disturbances but that people who do their work in these places are often also highly sensitized people.

9

Was That a Child Crying?

The old house by Bowker Creek, just across the street from Jean's own home at that time, looked as if it ought to be haunted. Its porch sagged dispiritedly and the paint was peeling. It was still, however, a handsome house, built sturdily upon rock. At one time it had been an old men's home, and the neighbours remembered a row of old men in dark trousers, white shirts and braces sitting in rocking-chairs on the veranda, rocking mindlessly hour after hour and staring wordlessly into space.

The children of the house were well known to Jean's son Kord; they used to play together quite often. They never played in the attic, however. The children would not go there, even after their father had installed a pool table and made the place bright and cheerful. They were also afraid to go up to the second storey alone, and favours and treats were given to pay for company on the journey upstairs. The two teenagers in the family would often offer to go to bed early, at the same time as the little ones; there seemed to be safety in numbers. Nobody had actually seen anything, however, and nothing out of the ordinary ever happened. It was simply that the second floor and the attic made them fearful.

When Jean heard about all this, she naturally paid the house a visit. She saw and felt nothing specific. The house seemed merely unpleasant and depressing. There was no sign of a haunting. Nevertheless, something was clearly wrong.

What *had* been wrong emerged a few days after she made her

visit. She bumped into Barbara Andrews, a friend whom she had not met since she had moved to this particular street. They talked of many unrelated things, and at parting they exchanged addresses. Barbara took one look at Jean's address and said, 'Good heavens! I used to live just a few doors away from you. In 1948 – in, you know, the old white house on the hill. The strangest thing that ever happened to me took place there, and after all these years it is just as plain and clear as if it had happened yesterday.

'I woke up one morning, sat up in bed and decided to indulge myself by reading a few more pages of my book. I was wide awake. I looked up and saw a small girl, about ten or eleven, standing at the foot of my bed. Her hair was blonde, long and cut in bangs, and she was wearing a nightgown, a long one with ruffles on the hem and at her wrists. Tiny blue flowers were printed on the material, which looked like flannelette. She was so sweet, with big blue eyes, freckles on her nose, a most lovely and enchanting child and beautifully cared for. As I watched, her eyes filled with tears, her lower lip protruded in a pout, and she turned and walked away from the end of my bed right through the wall. Jean, there was no door there!

'Later in the day my father checked the wall and was able to trace the faint outline of a door that had been boarded up. Do you know what a "safe room" is? It's a bedroom that can only be reached by going through the parents' room. It was for the unmarried daughters in the family, to keep them safe. Apparently this house had one of these at one time. Later, for convenience, the door between the bedrooms was closed and a new door was opened from the hallway.'

The safe room was characteristic of the American South, and a lot of Southerners came to Victoria during the years of Reconstruction after the Civil War, to avoid the unpleasantness. At one time Rockland Avenue consisted almost entirely of American mansions; the house may therefore have been affected by the emotions of survivors of the Civil War. At that time Victoria had many American immigrants; in fact, the most successful prostitute in Chinatown was a six-foot ex-slave who had been brought to Victoria and given her freedom.

Jean pondered the situation. The house was still very sad, but she had received no impression of a child ghost. She felt, indeed, that Barbara's sympathy for the girl, and the fact that after their encounter she had prayed for the spirit of the unhappy child, had probably released the ghost. The sadness, however, remained. It was probably the effect of all those old men, staring mindlessly into space, rocking their days away, that had caused the trouble, for this type of dream state often results in out-of-the-body experiences and the creation of thought forms without any intention on the part of the dreamer. In addition the house was built beside running water, which is always conducive to the creation of psychic disturbances, and upon rock, and rock, if it has decayed, becomes radio-active and gives off radon, one of the so-called 'noble' elements that is, according to physicists, extremely difficult to dispel, and radio-activity appears to be conducive to spiritual activity. It seems, indeed, that the house was being troubled by a combination of causes, and there was no single one that could be identified and tackled.

Child ghosts, imprisoned in a place and lost, unaware of anything but their own grief and confusion, are among the most pathetic of spectres. In the early 1970s Jean had one of her most disturbing experiences with them. She says:

'I was newly out of the closet as a witch, and as a reasonably intelligent and real-life witch I appeared on a lot of TV programmes and spoke on many radio talk-shows. During one talk-show a caller left her number with a request that I would phone her when we were off the air. She said she could not discuss the problem over the radio.

'Her name was Joan and she had a very strange story to tell. Her sister Violet, who lived alone, had a planchette, which she had been using for years. It sat on a small table in her living-room. Recently she had become aware that the planchette was moving of its own accord during the night, or when she went out. She placed a notebook on the table and began to copy its messages. At first all she received was a meaningless jumble of letters that only occasionally appeared to be forming real words. Then one day it spelt out the name Kozocari. Violet phoned a few trustworthy friends and asked if they knew anyone with this very unusual name. Within a week Joan heard me talking on CFAX radio. I was, of course, fascinated by this story but, like Joan and Violet, baffled.

'Several hours later Joan and Violet's cousin Fran phoned her from Seattle. Fran and Gerry had married very young and had begun a family immediately. A few months before the birth of their first child they found a small house that, miraculously, they could afford. The owners were very accommodating and went to a great deal of trouble to make sure that they could have the house. Cleaning and painting and getting started took all their time and energy, but soon they brought home their first little boy. Happy but exhausted, Fran frequently found her tiny baby cold, wet and crying, with the sheets and blankets on the floor, and his clothing in disarray, a condition quite impossible for a newborn baby to contrive himself. When I asked Fran why it didn't upset her more, she said she didn't know why: it just seemed as if she was not supposed to pay too much attention.

'As the years passed, seven children entered the family, and always the baby of the group was found in an impossible situation; the nursery was always in a mess. Carefully folded dry laundry would be found piled on top of the baby in the crib, and dozens of disposable diapers would be found shredded and thrown around the room, and even hanging from the light fixtures in the ceiling. Occasionally small scratches and bruises as if from pinching appeared on the baby.

'Each of the children had an imaginary friend of their own age and sex, and these they could conveniently blame their misdeeds upon. Fran said that sometimes these imaginary friends were so real that she could almost see them.

'With the birth of the seventh baby, a very special child in myth and legend, everything seemed to accelerate. Once the baby was found out of its crib and stuffed in a closet, scratched and bruised, and once it was discovered wrapped up in blankets, blue from near suffocation and bleeding from the nose. There were dozens of broken blood vessels on his face.

'Now Fran became really scared. This last incident had happened when all the older children were at school and she had been alone in the house. She was afraid of being accused of child abuse and knew that her story was too bizarre to be believed. As, crying and sobbing, she told all this to Violet and Joan, they looked at each other and said, "Call Jean!"

'The story was very strange, and it didn't fit into any of the usual patterns. The children were all too young to be the cause of poltergeist activity, and the house was quite new, so it was unlikely that it was a haunting. It was, however, intriguing and Fran obviously needed help. Fortunately an old friend from Toronto was visiting us. April Williams was an accomplished medium and had studied with good teachers, and I knew her work to be above reproach. Together we travelled to Seattle to visit Fran and her house.

'The situation had caused tension in Fran's marriage, so our investigation took place over a three-day period when the children were at school and her husband was at work. Over many pots of coffee we explored Fran's memory, listing everything that had happened. We left her smaller children with a neighbour and took Fran to lunch. Outside the house her memory seemed much clearer. She said, "I can't believe I've just let this go on and on. I've been living with this situation for over seven years." Fran and I stayed drinking coffee while April went back to the house alone. When we returned to the house over two hours later, April was sitting on the front steps, looking very pale and worried. She assured Fran that everything was fine and that we would return in the morning.

'We went back to our hotel, and April said, "I must have a bath and half an hour of meditation before I can tell you any part of what happened to me in the house." I bribed a waitress to bring us up a cup of salt for April's bath, and about three-quarters of an hour later April, calm and pale, began to tell her story.

'The house had been built and lived in by an elderly man

living alone with his aged mother. She was mildly psychotic, and he had never married but spent his life protecting and caring for her. As more homes were built around him, he made certain that nobody ever saw her or realized that she was living there. When he was convinced that he had a fatal disease he couldn't bear the thought of leaving her alone and so he killed her and himself. April had contacted him and redirected him and sent him to a better place, where he could find the friends and family of his childhood.

'I said, "It doesn't really explain all that has happened in the house, but everything is OK now, isn't it."

'April looked at me and said, "No. We have barely started."

'The house had been empty for many years after the murder – suicide. One day a middle-aged man moved in. He had a very expensive car and wore good clothes. Boxes arrived, but very little furniture. Heavy curtains covered the windows at night. Soon the neighbours became aware of a pattern. Several times a week two women would arrive in a taxi. Some hours later they would depart. One woman was always the same, an older, very plain, hard-faced woman who seemed almost to bully the young women who accompanied her. Sometimes people arrived late at night, and the lights of the house burned all night long. The house received no care; the paint peeled, the lawn grew dry and the grass sparse. Occasionally someone dug a little in the back garden, but if seeds were ever planted, no results were visible. No flowers bloomed. As April told me this, her voice faded away.

'I said, "April, what are you trying to tell me?"

'She said, "It was a house where illegal abortions were performed, and, Jean, the babies that were aborted grew up with the real children that lived in the house."

'I said, "April, I don't believe this. I really don't. It doesn't fit with any of my belief systems."

'She said, "It doesn't fit with mine either, but that's what I found there. Where do we go from here?"

'The next morning we talked to Fran and asked to speak with the older children one at a time, starting with the oldest. We asked them to tell us about their imaginary friends. They told us their names and their ages and explained that they were jealous of the living children who had parents and friends and family, which they had been denied.

'As we talked to the oldest child, Gerald, about his friend and enemy, Danny, I became aware of the same type of disassociation I had felt as a child during my first experience of a ghost at Muskoka. The feeling is almost that the adults are a different species and cannot possibly understand. Danny was always there, said Gerald, and generally getting him into trouble, but still very comforting when they were alone together. Danny said emphatically that all children have to have parents. He liked the times when Fran read to them and told stories; he was very unhappy when the family went to games because he was not comfortable when he was away from the house.

'Danny did not regard the other real children as friends or companions. He was concentrating upon Gerald. Though Danny and the other ghost children knew each other and would combine forces from time to time to create mischief, the real children could communicate only with their own particular ghost companions and not with the others. They did, however, know of their existence and would speculate about which ghost was responsible for this or that act of mischief. The ghost children claimed to dislike Fran and Gerry, but they seemed to enjoy intimate and cosy family occasions.

'Apparently a ghost child would attach himself or herself to a real child as soon as it had been born and returned from the hospital. At this stage the ghost child would be very angry and jealous, feeling that the real child had taken its place; this accounted for all the destruction in the nursery. Later the ghost children realized that they depended upon the real ones for their own existence and so formed an uneasy alliance with them.

'When Danny and the other older children had grown to feel comfortable about us and realized that we understood what they had been experiencing, we explained that their ghost companions had to be set free from the family and sent away. We asked each child to tell his or her particular ghost companion that someone kind and loving would come to take him or her to a place full of affection and happiness. Each ghost child told us, by way of his or her real counterpart, that someone had indeed come, and each described a child of the same sex, but a little older. We asked the two older ghost children to take the baby ones that were bonded to the three-, two- and one-year-old with them, and they agreed. When we spoke to the third and fourth children, they told us that the youngest ghosts had already left.

'When this was all over and we attempted to discuss the ghost children, the real children looked at us blankly. It was as if their memories had been wiped clean, and Fran said later that none of the children ever mentioned their imaginary friends again, although in the past they had been a constant subject of everyday conversation. After the sending-away of the ghosts the children behaved as if they had been relieved of an unpleasant chore.

'The sending-away of the ghost children occupied the whole morning and afternoon of our last day in Seattle, and when it was all done, Fran and April and I went to the local nursery and bought plants and a small cement statue of a cherub. Together we created a tiny memorial garden behind the house.

'Not long after the spirit children had been sent on their journey, Fran and Gerry completely changed their careers and moved out of the state. It seemed almost as if they had been kept there until the ghosts had all been set free.'

It was difficult for Jean to accept what had happened, for her beliefs had never led her to take the view that a foetus so incompletely developed that it could be safely aborted had a personality and could exist as a spiritual entity. There seemed, however, to be an explanation in the history of the house. It looked as if the suicide-murder in the house had created a kind of vortex into which spirits could be drawn and in which they could be imprisoned.

The first death had been matricide. The son had killed his mother. Significantly, the mother who had been murdered was mentally unbalanced, and therefore it is possible that she did not feel any change when her death occurred, and retained her possession of her son, not allowing him to leave. He had, in fact, joined her in death by his own suicide, and they had remained together imprisoned in the house. The mother murdered by her son had latched on to the children murdered by their mothers; the parallel is too clear to be avoided.

Whether or not this is the true explanation, this vortex effect is not uncommon. Indeed, it seems to have operated in the house on the hill of our first chapter. Vortices account for the way in which ghosts appear to attract each other. Where there is one ghost, others frequently follow, but, it seems, only when the first ghost is not merely a memory imprint but a presence, a spirit imprisoned or lost. Indeed, in many instances we have found it necessary to ask, at the beginning of an exploration, not only 'Who are you?' but 'How many of you are there?' Once the primary cause of the vortex has been removed, it is sometimes relatively easy to deal with later arrivals, though not always, for the most recent arrival may turn out to be the most resistant to persuasion. In dealing with ghosts, as in dealing with any group of people, there are very few absolute certainties.

When dealing with adult ghosts, one may quite reasonably command them to move on to the next plane of their own volition. Ghost children, however, cannot always to be relied upon in this way; many of them need a helper. This was the case with the little girl ghost whom Jean encountered.

The story began in a flea-market. Both Jean and I are avid frequenters of flea-markets. Our Sunday mornings are devoted to wandering from stall to stall, seeing what the spirit of serendipity will provide.

'One day,' Jean says, 'I made two wonderful finds, first Jessica North, who became my close friend, and secondly Arthur.

'Arthur, a pleasant young man in his middle twenties, asked if he could come and talk to me about the house he shared with two friends. Nancy and Tom, also in their middle twenties, were married and Arthur was single, and by sharing expenses the three of them were able to afford an attractive house in a part of Victoria near Beacon Hill Park that is called by the residents

"Cook Street Village". All three of them visited me and told me what had been happening.

'It had all begun with their house-warming party. It had started routinely, but as the evening wore on, tensions appeared, and a close group of friends became angry, aggressive and argumentative. Early the next morning the sound of running footsteps overhead woke Arthur, and when he turned on his bedside lamp, it hummed for a few seconds, then flared like a flash bulb. He heard a sound on the veranda roof, and a dull thud on the front steps. Thinking that someone was throwing rocks at the house, he went outside but found no sign of anything that could have caused the noises.

'The next morning Nancy described a recurring dream that she had had ever since moving into the house. In the dream a child was crying in the attic, and there were sounds of drunken laughter and music in the living-room. The dream always ended with the sound of breaking glass, and Nancy would wake up with her heart beating wildly and feeling terrified.

'Tom had heard rapid footsteps in the upper hallway, and sometimes the rocking-chair in the living-room seemed to move, but when he turned his head, it was always standing still. Tom and Arthur had climbed to the attic. There was no proper floor, only boards with loose insulating material. A small window gave light through an old lace curtain, and the net seemed to have dark brown stains. They suggested to Nancy that it might be hot chocolate, but both men thought privately that the stains were blood.

'A few days later a hard rubber ball was found on the stairs. It was about the size of a tennis ball, and the faded paint upon it was red, white and blue. When they tried to show the curtain from the attic to friends, they found it had disappeared. Dreams disturbed their sleep. Friends who visited them became angry and argumentative, and other friends failed to visit, although appointments had been made. Indeed, friends simply stopped coming to the house.

'While I made tea, they wandered round my house looking at the bric-à-brac I had picked up in the flea-markets, and then I heard Arthur let out a yelp, and he dropped a silver-framed picture on the floor. It was a photograph of my middle son, Kerry, in an old-fashioned tuxedo, sitting in a princess-style wicker chair surrounded by palm trees. The photograph had been posed to make it look as if it were a scene from a 1940s movie. I asked him why he had reacted in this way, and he said they had the same chair in the corner of their living-room, and it too had a palm tree beside it. Moreover, he frequently thought he saw a man sitting in it. He insisted that the man looked just like Kerry.

'We agreed to hold a seance in the house. When we arrived, about 9.30 in the evening, we found that a fourth person had moved in to share the house, and having been told the story, he had consented to join us in the seance. I sat in one corner while the four young people sat around the table in the middle of the room. They followed the usual rules, and we would tape-record the session. They would place their hands down on the table, left hand over right hand, forming a chain of hands that must under no circumstances be broken. If anyone became upset, he or she would alert the others by first asking for help or, if unable to speak, by twice pressing the neighbouring hands. Nothing was to be set on the table in case of psychic energy that could cause it to be thrown off or violently disturbed in some other fashion.

'They joined hands, and I lowered the lights and started the tape recorder. They were all very nervous. After a few minutes they asked if they could break the circle and have a drink of water. After the drink they re-formed the circle, changing around until they all felt more comfortable. Almost immediately after they had joined hands, the table began to rock. There were a few nervous giggles and whispers, and we discussed what was happening.

'Nancy and Arthur's hands, where they joined, began to glow with a pale blue light. We began to see sparks, and finally a gold spot of light appeared over Nancy's heart. Arthur's head sank forward until it almost reached the table. A moment later he straightened up and began to speak.

' "My Daddy went away to the war."

' "Who are you?' I asked.

' "My name is Beth."

' "How old are you."

' "I'm seven."

' "Who do you live with?"

' "Mummy, and sometimes Grammy comes to see me. Daddy's gone away."

' "What's your favourite toy?"

' "Daddy gave me a ball. I bounce it up and down the stairs."

' "Do you like ice-cream?"

' "We only have rice pudding now. We're rationed and there's no sugar and there's no butter."

' "What does your mother do?"

' "She's a telephone lady. She works at the office."

' "Who looks after you when she works?"

' "Abby. She lives next door. She's sixteen and she has a boy friend."

' "What are you doing here."

' "I'm waiting for Daddy. He said "Now, Princess, I want you to wait right here for me until I come back for you, and remember to do everything that mother tells you."

' "Do you do everything that mother tells you?"

'Arthur began to cry. His voice changed.

' "The bitch, the bitch! She has men here and she's keeping Beth in the attic. She gives her cocoa with sleeping-pills in it to keep her quiet. She doesn't want the men to know she has a child, because there are so many pretty single girls around. She said the competition was fierce and that she needed a new meal-ticket, since her husband had been killed. One night they were very drunk and they went to bed. Beth woke up and fell against the window, and it broke. She fell out, rolled down the veranda roof and fell down onto the steps. The neighbours heard the glass break and rushed out and found her, but she was dead. They had to wake up her drunken mother."

'Everyone round the table was now crying. I asked them to relax their hands very gradually and slowly draw apart.

'We discussed what had happened, and I explained that we must send Beth away, that her grandfather and grandmother would be waiting for her. The company wanted to keep her. She had touched their hearts and become a part of their lives. Arthur especially did not want to let her go. After much discussion they agreed to send the little ghost away, and I explained that they must be ruthless. If she refused to go, they must drive her away.

'They joined hands again, and Arthur began to talk to Beth and to tell us what her answers were.'

' "Beth, we want you to leave here."

' "I can't go."

' "Honey, you must go. Mummy, Daddy and Grandma are waiting for you."

' "I have to stay here. Daddy said he'd come back for me. I have to stay right here."

' "Beth, do you see a light? A nice warm light?"

' "Yes."

' "Daddy's there in the light. Go towards him."

' "I can't. He said to wait!"

' "How old were you?"

' "Four, almost five."

' "Beth, he told you to wait because you were just a little girl. Now you're a big seven-year-old girl. You're old enough to go to him. He'll come towards you, so you can see him. Can you see him, honey? Can you?"

' "Yes, I can."

'We all heard a rush of little footsteps across the ceiling towards the window, and we all cried.

'Newspapers from 1943 mentioned the accidental death of Mary Elizabeth, aged seven. Tom said we should have known it was a child; the roof was too low for an adult to run in the attic.

'Arthur phoned me several times over the next few weeks. They were giving up the house. Each time he talked to me he mentioned how much he missed Beth, and he wished he had not sent her away. Believing as I do in reincarnation, I think that Beth's father did come back for her and that it was he who set her free in his present incarnation as Arthur.

'I drove by the house last week. It was freshly painted and has new front steps. An elderly couple were working in the garden. The house looked comfortable and serene.'

10

Ghosts that Care and Guard

It is sometimes difficult to make a distinction between a ghost and a guardian spirit, for there are a number of recorded ghosts that have clearly seen their roles as those of protectors and even advisers. Sometimes, indeed, they constitute a kind of warning system. Few warnings, however, are as dramatic as the one which Jean came across when she was asked for advice about the experience of a night worker in a local sawmill.

It was the worker's wife, a hospital nurse and a colleague of Jean's husband, Sandy, who brought the matter up. She asked Sandy if Jean would advise her how to deal with something apparently supernatural that had happened to her husband. Jean agreed and, over coffee, the worker explained to her that he was on the night shift at the mill, working from midnight until eight in the morning. At about two o'clock he always took his supper at a long table; above his head a long pipe about two feet in diameter carried sawdust from a blower. One Monday as he was eating his supper alone in the lunch-room a terrible black shape chased him from the room. It was, he said, extraordinarily impersonal, like a person chasing away a goose. 'There was no emotion,' he said, 'only this time I was the goose.' He was afraid to go back to work, but when he told of his experience, his boss was unsympathetic and refused to allow him to change shifts. His friends and family accused him of just not wanting to work, but his wife was understanding. She realized that his fear was very real.

Jean suggested that he take a few days off, and said that she would meet him and his wife again the following Saturday. That Friday, at about 2.15 in the morning, the pipe carrying the sawdust became choked and burst, causing an explosion that destroyed the lunch-room, and the table at which the worker invariably sat was shattered into a pile of splinters. Jean says, 'I was given credit for saving his life, but what I was really doing was what I do best – procrastinating.'

Procrastination is not always without its uses. Indeed, Time is one of the ghost-hunter's most useful tools. It is important to have time on one's side so that one can investigate the situation immediately and interrogate people while the impressions are still fresh. It is even more important to be able to let a little time elapse before one takes action; undue haste may lead to encountering difficulties one has not anticipated. Sometimes, indeed, the ghost itself needs to have time to carry out a particular task. This appears to have been the case with the ghost of Mr Green.

Jean had last seen Mr Green at his daughter Shawna's wedding. It had been a happy time for the family. Shawna's twin sister had been the matron of honour, and one pew had been completely filled with her Girl Guide troop in full uniform. The only disquieting note was provided by the father of the bride, for his right hand was heavily bandaged and he was obliged to use his left one for all the handshaking that is obligatory at such ceremonies. He did his best to brush aside all anxious questions, however, and made light of the situation. He had suffered an accident while working on an electrical power line, and really there was nothing to be disturbed about. Nevertheless, from that time his health steadily deteriorated, and before many months were over he was confined to the downstairs den in his house, where his little floor-mop of a dog kept him company, and a year later he died.

It was three years after Mr Green's death that his widow asked Jean to advise her about strange happenings in the house. Jean did not ask for details at that time but went along to the house with her daughter Tara and Cece and Betty, two of her favourite companions on such expeditions. She told them nothing about the house or the family.

It was a cool, clear evening after a warm day when they set out for the tall, square house and made their way up the sweeping driveway to the *porte-cochère*, admiring the architecture. Mrs Green welcomed them into the house and told them to go anywhere they pleased and do anything they thought necessary. The inside of the house was as attractive as the exterior. The downstairs living-room contained a wide frieze of beautifully moulded fruit that had been created by the first owner, a woman artist who had a studio at the back and whose fear of fire had led her to include no fireplaces in the building. The upstairs bedrooms each contained marble wash-basins and antique plumbing.

The investigators had each brought dowsing rods with them, and they walked slowly round the lower floors of the house, each taking a different route. In the den they all experienced a distinct response. One rod also reacted in the living-room and two by the back door. One of the group refused to go down into the basement but the two who did venture there experienced no reaction from their rods.

As they moved upstairs, they experienced reactions on the fifth stair from the bottom, on the stair landing and in two places in the upper hallway. At this point Mrs Green elected to try out a dowsing rod herself and went into the rear bedroom. The rod reacted with such force that it twisted her arm completely and unbalanced her. Jean had to catch her to prevent her from falling, and the rod was gripped so tightly in her fist that the fingers had to be prised open.

After this initial exploration was over, the visitors asked for details of the disturbances that had occurred. They had begun almost immediately after Mr Green's death three years previously. Cold spots were felt in the den where he had spent so much time during his illness, and it had eventually become so uncomfortable that it was rarely used. Cold spots had also been felt in the living-room, where his favourite chair had been placed, on the stairway, near the back door and in the upper hall and rear bedroom. It seemed that the dowsing rods had been quite precise in their signals.

An actual spectre had been seen only once. The front door had opened and a grey whirlwind had rolled and roared down the hallway, through the kitchen and out of the back door, leaving both doors open. This was seen, heard and felt quite distinctly, and the route the whirlwind had taken was exactly the one Mr Green had always taken when returning from work. He himself had not believed in psychic phenomena, ironically enough, though the rest of the family were all psychically sensitive and had experienced some instances of extra-sensory perception.

At this time the house was up for sale. Mr Green had intended to sell the house when his children were grown up, and so his widow had followed his wishes and put it on the market. Nobody appeared to be interested in it, however, and there was a feeling that maybe prospective buyers were being put off by the atmosphere in the house itself. Jean agreed that this could be the case, and she and her companions also agreed that the house was certainly haunted. They offered to exorcize it, to contact Mr Green and send him on his way. The family, however, were hesitant. They had loved the man very much and did not feel it was right to put him out of his own home. No exorcism was performed.

Over the next few months the house became more and more uncomfortable, and it became obvious that it would never find a purchaser, so it was withdrawn from the market.

In August the following year Mrs Green was getting ready to go to Britain on a visit when the disturbances became even more intense. A large brass door-knocker that had been mounted on a piece of wood fell off a four-inch-wide plate rail in the den: it had been sitting there safely for twelve years. Three plaster mermaids fell off the bathroom wall and smashed into smithereens. A picture of the children fell down in the hall and was found leaning carefully against the wall, the glass unbroken. All these objects had been Mr Green's personal belongings. The knocker was remounted on its piece of wood and put back on the plate rail; the next morning it was discovered sitting on a love-seat six feet away.

This kind of disturbance is often due to poltergeists, but there were no children of the correct age to produce poltergeist activity, and nobody in the family was a practical joker or would be inclined to do anything to upset Mrs Green.

About four years after Mr Green's death an old army buddy of his returned to Victoria. They had served together and remained good friends when they came back to Canada at the end of the war. Their marriages did nothing to disrupt their friendship, and the two couples became a foursome. As time passed, however, the arrival of children and the demands of separate careers had separated them, and they had drifted apart. Now Mr Green was dead and his old friend was divorced and lonely and delighted to renew his friendship with Mrs Green. They soon became close companions and decided to get married.

During this period of the renewal of a friendship and of growing intimacy, the haunting continued but with lessened energy. It seemed almost as if Mr Green felt obliged to make his presence felt only when something of which he did not approve occurred.

On the morning of Mrs Green's wedding the women of the family having been to their hairdressers, met in the bride's bedroom to dress. Mrs Green was sitting at her dressing-table adjusting her flowers when all heard a dry cough, the very sound which they had heard so often during the last days of Mr Green's life. They turned and again saw the grey whirling column beside them in the room. It remained there for only a few moments; then they heard a great sigh as it dispersed and drifted away like mist.

Mr Green was never heard from again. The house was sold almost immediately, and the newlyweds lived a happy and contented life undisturbed by any further activities on the part of the new husband's old army friend. It appears that he had been watching over the house, perhaps even urging his wife towards finding another husband. His duty done, he could leave.

A number of ghosts appear to have tasks to perform, and they tend to disappear when their duties are done. Some, however, do not know when their tasks have been completed; this was the case with a ghost in Esquimalt, which Jean was asked to investigate.

It was quite a small house, and a woman and her two children were the only inhabitants. They were more puzzled than distressed, and also just a little irritated, for something was going on which they did not understand, and it was a nuisance. There was only one kind of disturbance. It took place regularly, however. Outside the bathroom door, in the ceiling, there was a trapdoor leading to a small attic, and every evening at dusk, and as early as 4.30 p.m. in the winter and as late as 8.30 p.m. in the summer, they would find the trapdoor gaping open. It would also be found open in the early mornings as the children were getting ready for school, or even earlier during the summer. This did not alarm anyone or cause any distressed feelings, but it was a nuisance, for the trapdoor was too high to be closed without the use of a ladder, and in the winter it was especially bothersome, for the woman felt that the heat of the house was escaping and she was having to go and get the ladder every morning and evening from outside the house, for the place was too small to keep the ladder indoors. She tried ignoring the problem and leaving the trapdoor open, but this made her feel uncomfortable. Her discomfort was increased by her seeing what she called a UFO floating just outside her kitchen window. It was shaped like a huge cupped hand.

Jean discussed the phenomena with Dr Max Edwards of the University of Victoria, for he was working on a theory linking poltergeist activities to UFO sightings. The children were, however, much too young to be the cause of poltergeist activity, for this is usually caused by those on the edge of puberty: moreover, at this time the use of hallucinogenics was fashionable, and it seemed to Jean that the cupped hand might well 'have more to do with LSD than PSI'.

Still, Jean went to the house with Marion George and Alan Bruce, who both carried their dowsing rods. One or two others came along to share the experience. The children were out of the house that evening, and the house felt perfectly all right.

Thermometer readings were taken, the dowsing rods were put to use, and there was no sign of any supernatural activity whatsoever.

Marion George had to leave early because of baby-sitting problems, and the company went to the front door with her to bid her goodnight. When they turned around, the trapdoor had opened. The men went outside and got the ladder and climbed up and examined the tiny attic with their flashlights. There was nothing to be seen but a round window that had been boarded up and a great deal of dust. One of the men then carefully closed the trapdoor, and the group left the house, slamming the front door as hard as they could, and ran heavily up and down the outside stairs several times, to see if this kind of activity could be responsible for causing the trapdoor to come open. Jean believes strongly that one should always seek a logical physical explanation of odd happenings before attempting to find a psychic one. The trapdoor did not open.

Summer is the best time to ask questions of neighbours, for they tend to be outside their houses, weeding their gardens or cutting hedges, and it is possible to start a conversation easily, whereas in the winter one has to knock on doors and ask questions and seem very much more of an intruder. The neighbours told Jean that the previous owner had been an elderly gentleman with a Scottish name and accent. He was a quiet man and lived there for fifteen years until his death. He had raised pigeons. Early every morning and at dusk every evening they would fly down the street with a great whirring of wings and come to the house and enter the round window in the attic. When all the pigeons were home, the old gentleman would close the window to keep his friends safe from marauding cats.

That evening Jean returned to the house and asked if she could be given a half hour alone in the little attic. It did not take her long to do what was necessary, but she indulged herself by spending a few moments alone with the gentle soul before explaining to him that his friends no longer needed attention, that all was well with him and them and that he could depart and complete his passage to the next plane.

The trapdoor never opened again. The kindly neighbours said quietly to Jean, 'It is strange. The pigeons left the morning of the day he died and never returned. And oddly enough we never see pigeons on this street any more.'

The house presented no more problems after that, and when Jean talked to the householder neither of them mentioned the UFO. Nevertheless, the UFO also had to have an explanation and, in thinking the whole matter over afterwards, it appeared to Jean that the hand was cupped in just the fashion a hand would be cupped if it were offering seed to birds.

The house was pulled down shortly afterwards in order to make way for a development, and it is good to think that the old Scotsman had been sent comforted away before this happened.

Some houses are more blessed than troubled by ghosts. Jean herself has lived in several haunted houses and, she says, 'Three of them were pleasantly haunted. One house on Harrison Street seemed to be a loving haven for children. In the years we lived there, our three children had absolutely no health problems, not even a cold or a sniffle. Our fourth child, Kord, was conceived in the house, and he is a charmed child and has been surrounded all his life by good friends.

'The first manifestation in the Harrison house took place late on a Saturday afternoon just as dusk was falling. Kerry and Kevin had received their allowances already, but our daughter Tara was a spendthrift, and her allowance would be spent fifteen minutes after she received it. Therefore we made a new arrangement – a bank-account system. She was given a credit of 50 cents and had to ask for cash and explain why she needed it. She was a very independent child, and this really broke her heart, and we were also distressed. On this occasion she turned away to hide her tears and went towards the stairs, a steep flight which led up to a blank wall. Suddenly we heard a sound like a pebble dropping. Something hit the fourth step from the top and slowly bounced down and landed at Tara's feet. It was a very old, very shiny dime. It was also so hot that Tara dropped it when she picked it up.

'Another incident concerned our fourth child, Kord. After he was born, he was placed in the middle of the three upstairs bedrooms. I would frequently go into his room in the morning and find it full of the scent of a freshly smoked cigarette. My husband, Sandy, always insisted that he had not been smoking in the child's room and had, indeed, slept soundly the whole night.

'During the day Kord would wake and begin to cry, and I would start to warm his bottle before going upstairs to get him, when I would hear a sound like "Sshhh sshhh", and when I went to pick him up he would always be laughing and cooing and turning his head to look at someone I couldn't see.

'When I enquired about the house's history, I learned that it had once been a boarding-house, and Kord's room had been occupied by an old gentleman. One night while smoking in bed he had thrown a cigarette out of the window and set fire to the roof. The very next day he was bundled off to the veterans' hospital, where he died within six months. When I told this story to my husband, who worked in the hospital, he recalled caring for the old gentleman during his last days. I love the way in which this kind old gentleman came back to cheer up a heartbroken little girl and to help a tired mother care for her new baby. We were sure he was responsible, for from time to time we had glimpsed out of the corners of our eyes an old gentleman in a gold-coloured sweater moving about the garden.'

When living in Red Deer, Alberta, Jean had a young friend who was a great help to her. Margaret Redhead was a sixteen-year-old native girl. Kind and loving, she was completely overshadowed by her beautiful sister and a clever older brother. She herself was homely and not particularly sturdy, but she was Jean's favourite of the three children, so when Jean developed health problems while awaiting the birth of her third child, Margaret was the one person she wanted to be with her.

Jean says, 'We talked, knitted and gossiped as we waited. Under medication to keep me quiet, I often said, "Promise me that you will stay with me for two weeks after the baby is born." I knew that I would be in a state of confusion because of the excessive medication I had been given, and I was afraid I might neglect the other children. Margaret always laughed and said, "Come hell or high water, I'll stay for two weeks."

'The baby, Tara, arrived on 28 January, pale and blonde but with the strange light brown eyes that all my children are born with. That weekend Sandy was home, and Margaret asked if she could visit her family. I said, "Yes, but ..." and she laughed and said, "I know, I know! I promise I'll come back and stay with you for two weeks."

'Monday arrived and Sandy went to work, leaving me alone with the baby and the two other children. There was a knock at the door, and I hurried to let Margaret in, eager to hear all the gossip. Instead of Margaret, my landlady stood there, looking very uncomfortable. "I don't know how to tell you," she said. "I've never had to do this before, but Margaret is dead. She went to sleep about 1 a.m. on Sunday night and when they went to wake her on Monday morning she was dead." An aneurism while she slept had ended Margaret's brief sixteen-year-life.

'The baby slept until Sandy arrived, along with a nurse friend who wanted to see the baby. After scolding me for not calling her "Alexandra" after her father, she bustled into the nursery and returned carrying a tiny dark-skinned, black-haired baby. Quickly changing her, she said, "How cute! What a sweet little baby, darling little Margaret!" I was sure that I had somehow lost my mind. The heavy medication given women with problem pregnancies at that time had, I knew, somewhat disoriented me. I thought that if I said anything they would lock me up. Therefore I remained silent, wondering bemusedly what had happened to *my* baby, Tara.

'All the visitors who came to see our new baby automatically called her Margaret. No one ever asked what her name was; they just called her Margaret. The sweet little dark-haired baby was very placid and made my life very easy. Everyone mentioned that she did not look like anyone in our family.

One morning I went to the cradle, and there once again was my blonde, fair-skinned Tara. I picked her up, and Tara she has been ever since. Weighing her and entering the results on the calendar, I realized that Margaret had died exactly two weeks previously. Then I understood: Margaret had come back and helped me during those two weeks, carrying out her promise in the only way she was able, in the body of my baby. Nobody ever called the baby Margaret again.'

These three adventures clearly tell us that not all ghosts are trouble-makers. Indeed, Jean says that there may sometimes be advantages in living in a haunted house, although in general it is not wise.

'In the three unhaunted houses in which we lived,' she says, 'nothing of any importance was accomplished. Life seemed dull and boring. Haunted houses become batteries that magnify whatever is in the atmosphere. Pessimism, fear or negativity will be amplified by the energy expended by the inhabitants. A deliberate switch can, however, be made. Negativity can become positive creative energy. If a ghost is perceived to be frightening or depressing, it will only become more so. To me a ghost appearance in the house is a sign of a powerful energy force. If it is greeted as a sign of positive energy, it can then accelerate and amplify everything you do in the house; whatever talents or creativity you possess will grow like a healthy plant. As beauty is considered to be in the eye of the beholder, so too the atmosphere of a haunted house can be a way of tapping into the greater universe of positive power. A haunted house is a place of energy. I have never been frightened in a haunted house. I have been amused and bemused and confused and bewildered but I have never been frightened.'

Mr Green, the pigeon-fancier, and the old gentleman in the gold-coloured sweater were certainly not frightening. Indeed, perhaps they should be labelled not ghosts but guardian spirits, after all.

11

Ghosts Don't Have To Be Dead

In the minds of most people, the word 'ghost' immediately suggests an apparition of someone dead, or perhaps an apparition that is a representation of events or emotions long past. By no means all apparitions fit this description, as we have already seen in the case of the Red Devil, whose 'ghost' performed its manoeuvres while he was still very much alive.

Another instance of astral travel in which a live person transmits his or her image to another place is that of the old lady in Fairfield. Jean tells the story.

'We were house-hunting,' she says, 'and the real-estate lady had made an appointment for us to see a house in Fairfield. The street was wide, with well-kept lawns and sidewalks, and there was a very prominent "For Sale" sign on the front lawn. The house, however, had very little character, the only interesting detail being an inglenook in the living-room. The owners escorted us upstairs, around the living-room and downstairs into the basement.

'As the five of us, the owners of the house, my husband and I, and the lady from the real-estate office, formed a small parade, it was apparent that we were the only people in the house. When we came back upstairs from the basement, a grey-haired older lady was sitting at the kitchen table shelling peas into a cream-coloured enamel colander. She wore black sensible laced shoes, white ankle-socks, a faded print dress covered with an old grey nylon sweater. She wore a hairnet covering thin curls. The man and lady of the house pointed out several special features in the kitchen, completely ignoring the lady. When we left the kitchen after a few minutes, I was still furious at the rudeness that had been shown the elderly lady, who was obvious someone's mother or grandmother.

'We stood on the sidewalk talking to the sales lady and telling her that we were really not at all interested in the house. As she continued her sales pitch, I turned away and gazed across the street at a building bearing a sign explaining that this was an old people's home. Sitting in a bay window, in a wheelchair, staring across the street at the house we had just left, was the lady I had seen in the kitchen. Technically, it was probably a case of astral projection. Longing for the independence of having her own home, and dreaming, her astral body was able to travel into the house and for a few minutes take control of her life. There had been nothing ghostly or transparent about the lady I had seen shelling peas. She was absolutely and completely real, but I was the only one of the five of us who had seen her.'

Astral projection of this kind can be, and indeed usually is, wholly unintentional, though we must again remember the case of the Red Devil.

Another example of this phenomenon involves a young man with whom Jean had been working very hard on his healing abilities. He bought Jean a record. She did not want to play it with him there because then it might become 'our song' and acquire an undue significance. She therefore left it to one side, intending to play it some other time, when the young man was not present. When one is working with people on their psychic abilities, emotional complications can occur as a result of the intimate nature of the teaching and learning process, and Jean is always careful to avoid any romantic bonding of this kind.

The next morning she put the record on the record-player, and as she was gazing idly at the front door, the young man's shape appeared there. As the music continued, the shape grew stronger and more definite before it disappeared. Later that evening, as Jean was talking to the young man on the phone about the record, she asked him, 'What were you doing at 9.20?'

and he said, 'I was in the second level of my meditation.'

Sometimes one can, quite unintentionally, leave an image of this kind behind one in a place. Some years ago, when visiting Toronto, I would make use of the spare bed in the apartment of a woman friend in Kensington Market. We got on well together. There was no stress, and we shared many interests. After one particular visit, however, she told me, on the phone, that I must find other lodging for my next visit. I felt a little hurt, as well as surprised, and asked her why. She told me that the day after I had flown back to Victoria, and for several days following, there had been a ghostly companion in the house, an entity that she perceived as a white shape, and she knew that it was something I had left behind me. I had not, during my last visit, done anything extraordinary; there had been no times of emotional stress or even anxiety. I could not understand it, but it does seem that for a week or so there I too was a ghost.

I was myself totally unaware of having left any presence behind me in Toronto. I had no message that I was aware of wishing to send. The ghost of the young woman in Beacon Hill Park, however, quite certainly did have a message, and at the time it was seen the person it represented was equally certainly alive.

The spectre wore white slacks and was deeply tanned, with long blonde hair, and appeared in some bushes on the side of the hill screaming silently as she held out her arms in a gesture of terror. She was usually seen in the summer, but this may be simply because the park is more frequented in the summer and therefore there are more observers.

Eight years after the ghost's first appearance, the body of a missing woman was found in that very grove of bushes on the side of the hill. The missing woman was wearing dark jeans and had pale skin and long dark hair. Spectres do sometimes appear as photographic negatives, and often it is the negative form of a photograph taken in a haunted house that provides a significant image, as it did in the case of the house on the hill. She had appeared as a negative. This murder has never been solved, and each 2 June Jean places flowers on the spot where the spectre appeared for eight years before her death. (2 June appears to be a deadly date for beautiful young women with long dark hair in Victoria. Three have disappeared on this date, and only one of them has ever been found.)

The screaming ghost of Beacon Hill Park foretold the future. It is hard to determine, however, whether the young woman herself, by a kind of astral projection, was foreseeing her own murder or whether, by a curious twist in time, the place pre-recorded a memory before the event had occurred.

Places do seem certainly, to be able to record memories without, apparently, the assistance of any human intermediary. Victoria provides an excellent example of this phenomenon, for sometimes in October the two blocks of Shelbourne Street, just south of the Hillside shopping mall, undergo a strange transformation. Between two and three o'clock of a Sunday morning, the commonplace street lined with houses, shops and small businesses becomes a gravel road, fringed only by trees and bushes. Grass grows down the middle, bordered by tyre tracks. This is usually seen by people who are driving alone, and they are sure that somehow they have taken a wrong turn. Suddenly, however, they are at Hillside and surrounded by lights. The really strange thing is that, even though it is October, springtime broom and bulrushes line that country road.

A long straight stretch of road on the way from Victoria to Sooke called China Flats is also haunted. It is a pretty place, with the skeleton of an old barn by a grove of trees forming a backdrop. Bob and Charlene Stallings had driven the road many times, but this particular night in 1978, in the shadowy twilight it made them very nervous. Their nerves were already stretched, because Charlene's mother had died about three weeks before, and their grief was like a dull toothache. Until this evening they had managed to keep their minds occupied, by being busy dealing with the problems caused by the death.

As they drove along, Bob became suddenly aware that his breathing had changed and become very shallow and loud; the hair on the back of his head tingled, and he was sure that there was somebody in the back seat of the car. He told his feeling to Charlene, who said, 'I know, but I'm afraid to look.' They found themselves whispering to each other, and both had the conviction that they had a supernatural being for a passenger.

Bob said, 'Do you think it's your mother?'

Charlene said, 'No, because I wouldn't be this frightened if it was mother.'

'Shall we stop?' said Bob.

'Is it a ghost or is it a real person. And how did it get in the car?' she replied.

The conversation continued in whispers as they wondered whether it was a ghost or a real person, and then, as suddenly as the presence had arrived, it was gone. Bob pulled in to the side of the road. The whole experience had lasted only five minutes, but when it was over, the fear remained.

Three days later Jean was doing her regular stint as a guest on Joe Easingwood's radio talk-show, talking about ghosts. Charlene phoned in on the hot line and was able to get through on her first try, which was very unusual. When she began to tell her story, the computer/switchboard lit up like a Christmas tree as caller after caller told a similar story. At last an old-timer told of a Chinese farmer trying to get to Colwood to find a doctor for his dying wife. Car after car refused to stop. In anguish, he stepped in front of an oncoming car, trying to make it stop, and was killed instantly. When the police went to his home, they found that his wife was dead. Fifty years later he was still trying to reach help. Did he know at some point that his wife was already dead, and commit suicide?

It seems clear that, like houses, roads remember. Just past Christie Point, under a railway trestle, the highway curves gently as it begins to climb a small hill. On the left, about halfway up the hill, is a small pub. Since 1940 people driving this quiet road have had to ram on their brakes to avoid hitting a large dog crossing the road towards the pub. On looking closer, it is seen to be a man with black hair falling over his forehead so that his features are obscured. He wears a long khaki army greatcoat and crawls slowly, as if in great pain. Some car-drivers stop to go to his aid, but always the spectre fades away. Had he been beaten and was he crawling to the pub for help? Or was the poor soldier so inebriated that he couldn't walk? As he is always seen by people in cars, it is likely that he was the victim of a car accident.

Another spectral jay-walker has been seen on a road in Saanich, where there is also the ghost of a complete house. The house was built by Mary and Stephen Sandover. It was a gracious place, with land stretching down to the sea, a beautiful apple orchard fed by a crystal spring, and a lawn and garden surrounding an exquisite house. Special wooden fretwork finishings came from San Francisco. Next door to them Mary's brother John built an identical house; side by side, the twin houses and the two families lived in harmony. John was blessed with children and grandchildren, and the house was always full of life's joys and sorrows. Mary and Stephen lived out their lives expending all their love on the orchard and the house, for they had no children. When Mary died, Stephen sold the property piece by piece, until at last all that remained was the house and a few fruit trees growing around the well. People at the experimental farm that was built upon what had been Sandover property often saw Stephen digging in the vicinity of the well, but nothing was ever planted there, and nothing ever grew.

After Stephen's death in the late 1930s, his bank books and cash were never found, although he had received large sums for his property and had lived a very frugal life. The house and property were searched again and again. During the Second World War it was a boarding-house for the wives of airmen at the Pay Bay Airport. Later it was purchased by the school board, and the house was boarded up and left to rot.

People began to complain about a shadowy figure that crossed the road in front of their cars, causing them to stop suddenly to avoid an accident. Jumping out of the car to confront the person or shadow, they found no one was ever there, and there were no adjacent bushes where anyone could have hidden.

The teenagers in the neighbourhood discovered the house and soon found a way to enter it. While their friends remained outside, one would run upstairs to Mary's room, whereupon the room would light up with a strange greenish light. Then they would run down the stairs and outside, hoping to be quick enough to see the light before it faded. During the day adults dug around the well and in the flower beds, hoping to find the canning jars and milk cans in which they believed Stephen had hidden his fortune. The house was finally torn down as a hazard, but the children said they could still see it, a black shadow outlined by a green glow, with one bright window.

Still the shadowy figure brought cars to a halt in the road before the house. The house's twin still stood and sheltered a family, its roof neat and its paint shining.

One night Jean and her friends went to see the ghost house and easily found the cement outlines, but unfortunately a bright street light had been erected at that very spot, apparently because this part of the road had been judged a traffic hazard, and it was now impossible to see the spectral house. As they returned to the car, a shadow crossed the road, and Jean understood why nobody had ever found Stephen's fortune. The shadow crossed the road not towards the house but away from it.

The property is now the Panorama Leisure Center, and Stephen's fortune is therefore encased in cement and will probably never be found.

Three teenage boys who had often visited the house returning from a fishing trip at three in the morning one summer, being aware of the ghostly activity, slowed down as they passed the place where the house had stood. About a quarter of a mile further on, they passed a little old lady in a long dress and a sunbonnet trudging down the road, a long rope held in her hand and passed over her shoulder, and at the end of it was an emaciated old man with long, straggly hair and beard. He wore overalls over long-sleeved underwear. The strange figures paid no attention to the passing car. The teenagers told their story to an old-timer, who said that in about 1910 'Aunt Emma's husband went mad, and so she locked him up in the attic, and on nights when there was no moon at all she would take him out for a walk on a long rope, like a dog on a leash.' Unfortunately, we do not know who 'Aunt Emma' was, so this ghost remains unexplained.

Memory imprints of this kind are often observed, and they should not disturb anyone unduly. In my own house on Victoria

Avenue we were haunted by just such a ghost. I do not know who first came across it. I myself, on going to the bathroom in the middle of the night, would sense a shadowy presence in the corridor. Sometimes it was so close that I felt obliged to murmur 'Excuse me' as I brushed past. I had the same sensation that everyone has when they feel, but do not see, someone standing behind them. The ghost was, I sensed, a quite young girl, not very tall, and possibly Chinese or Eurasian. I did not mention her to the children, or to our house-guest whose room was at the end of the corridor.

Our guest was working a late shift at the Oak Bay Beach Hotel, and so we would leave the upper corridor light on when we went to bed, so that he would not have to make his way in the dark. One afternoon, before setting out for work, he said, apropos of nothing, 'You know, there's no need to leave the light on for me. I know my way, and I'm quite used to the ghost.' It was then that we discovered that our daughter Alison was also used to the ghost. It would follow her along the corridor to her room at the other end of the corridor quite regularly, but it never went in.

We lived quite contentedly with our ghost until one morning Glen, our house-guest, reported that the previous night he had woken up to see her standing by his bed, a teenage girl, completely naked. He switched on the light and she was gone. When he switched the light off again, however, she reappeared. He fell asleep with the light on.

This was, we felt, going a little too far, and Jean, Sylvia, Alison and I gathered in Glen's room one evening and spoke firmly to her. She has not appeared so blatantly since and, indeed, seems, if not to have gone away entirely, at least to have become a great deal less intrusive. We have not been able to find out anything about her. We think she may have been a servant in the days when big Oak Bay houses all had servants, but we cannot be sure.

Nobody can be sure, either, about another young lady who haunts, or at least partly haunts, Craigdarroch Castle. One day a workman repairing the old building phoned Jean to tell her about his experiences on the third floor. After eating his lunch, seated in a comfortable chair facing the stairway, he relaxed and became a little drowsy. A movement on the stairs caught his attention. A small satin shoe and the trail of a long skirt and about twelve inches of a lady's gown were slowly descending the stairs. He watched the train of the skirt slide silently across the stairs and then drop straight down as if weighted to continue the slow slide to the edge of the next stair. The silence and the slow motion fascinated him for several minutes. A sound caught his attention, and when he looked back, it was gone. Jean always calls this 'the One Foot Ghost', because the workman saw only a foot or so of the gown. 'Where was the rest of her?' she asks, and thinks it was the memory imprint of a young girl in her first long gown concentrating on walking like a lady and not tripping on her skirt.

This ghost would frighten nobody, and, indeed some ghosts are positively endearing. Jean once experienced such a ghost, but it was not a human one. She tells the story:

'Sin was our Siamese cat, one of a very special breed. Her favourite time was just before dinner, because during its preparation she was able to talk us into giving her shreds of meat and cheese, but dozens of times I had stepped on her poor tail. Each time I felt it scrunch beneath my feet I felt sick, but she was never hurt, nor was she resentful. Otherwise a very friendly cat, she several times snapped at the young children who were visiting us. Fearing for the safety of the children, I arranged to give her to a nice couple, who wanted to mate her with their male. Eventually we would receive a kitten. Three weeks later, while preparing supper, I felt the familiar awful feeling of my foot on the cat's tail. "Dammit, Sin, keep out of my way," I said, and, looking down at the empty floor, I realized that something was very wrong. Calling the people to whom I had given her, I said, "What has happened to Sin?"

"We didn't want to tell you. She got out this morning and was run over by a car. How did you know?"

'I replied, "She just came by to say goodbye."

'I hung up and said a special blessing on my small faithful friend.'

Ed Gould, a local gossip columnist, and his wife Jan, shared their home near the Ross Bay Cemetery with a delightful ghost. Each night their sleep was interrupted at 4.20 a.m. by a cat jumping on the bed, kneading the covers into a comfortable nest, settling down and purring contentedly. The cosy warmth soon sent the Goulds back to sleep, and when they awoke each morning a small, round, warm depression was mute testimony to their spectral visitor.

No cat-lover would, I think, wish to exorcize a cat ghost. My daughter Brigid certainly has no intention of exorcizing hers. This summer she moved into a semi-detached house and had some difficulty in persuading the landlord that she could keep her cat, Tigger. The landlord said that some earlier tenants had owned a cat that had been a real nuisance, but he eventually agreed that Tigger was acceptable. On moving in, Brigid kept Tigger in the house, to prevent him running back to his old home; all the doors and windows were firmly shut. She was therefore a little surprised to glimpse a grey cat wandering in the hallway and then disappearing suddenly. She said nothing about this, but then her boy friend said that he had seen a grey cat. Since that first sighting they have both seen the grey cat several times both upstairs and downstairs. What surprises them both is that Tigger does not seem to have noticed it at all, as cats are commonly regarded, with justice, as being hypersensitive where psychic phenomena are concerned. But in this cats are like people: some are more attuned to these things than others. And perhaps it is just as well that not everyone sees ghosts.

Appendix: A Rite of Exorcism

The following rite of exorcism is never carried out slavishly, for different problems require different emphases. It has, however, been used many times and has proved effective, as some of the narratives in this book have revealed.

If the place is unfamiliar, one should make a preliminary visit during the daytime, as blocks are frequently put in the exorcist's way; last-minute emergencies, unexpected visitors or phone calls often happen.

Exorcisms are usually held in the evening after dusk, and most usually around 9 p.m. The day's excitements are over, the house enters into its own in the darkness, and people are more sensitive to psychic influences.

The householders themselves should be present, but most usually we find that only one of the couple who own the house will attend. This is likely to be the woman of the house, who prefers to arrange a time for the ceremony when her man is somewhere else. On the whole women handle these matters better than men.

The householders are always asked to have one or two friends with them for the exorcism. These friends should be sympathetic, caring and close. They must also, obviously, be open-minded and sensitive to the feelings of others. In most instances there are only two or three friends who fit the bill, and this is around the right number. One emphatically does not need a crowd.

Jean usually takes two of her students with her, students who know what they are doing, so that they can perform the main binding and sealing ceremony. She also likes to have somebody there who has a great deal of power and who is able to keep a general eye on the situation and on the emotional states of the people there, while she herself is concentrating all her energies upon the rite itself.

The gathering therefore includes four visitors: Jean herself, two assisting students and another person. I myself have been that person on several occasions.

The rite of exorcism is a very intimate matter, and not something one wishes a great many people to observe. Indeed, the larger the group, the more difficult it is to ensure that everybody is concentrating their attention upon the work that is being done.

The whole ceremony should be written out on cards, because sometimes the atmosphere is so overwhelming that one may lose one's place. The ceremony must be carried out in the proper order, and once begun, except in quite extraordinary circumstances, it must be completed. One must not, however, worry so much about the exact words as to lose one's concentration and confidence if one mispronounces something or fluffs. The intent and the nature of the gesture are more important than anything else.

In an exorcism, too, it is important that all present are absolutely at one for the crucial parts of the ritual. Therefore at some point it is wise to ask the group if everyone is prepared for the ritual to proceed to completion.

Perhaps here I might comment on the doggerel quality of many of these verses used in spells and rituals. It is important that such verses can be easily memorized and that they do not involve any great intellectual concentration. Their nursery-rhyme quality moreover tends to appeal, at a deep level, to almost everybody, for such rhymes are in everybody's background, and once in our childhood we found it easy to assent to and accept the simplicities of jingling rhymes. Moreover, doggerel of this kind is rather chanted than spoken; one does not recite 'Mary, Mary, Quite Contrary' in the same way one recites a Shakespearean sonnet or a poem by Robert Frost. Of course, not all ritual verses and spells are of this kind, for some carry with them the necessity of meditating and concentrating upon a particular problem and visualizing it with clarity and with intellectual precision. The more particular and individual the problem, the more sophisticated is the speech needed, but when one is dealing less with matters of detail and more with the over-all intent, the gesture matters more than the content. Moreover, one feels a certain security and confidence in words whose simplicities have lasted through the ages – or, at least, feel as if they have done so.

One must also realize that in conducting an exorcism one is opposing forces whch may be very strong indeed and that one is, of necessity, doing this in a fairly short space of time. Therefore one must not clutter up one's mind with subtleties and nuances but swiftly, and surely, deal with necessities by way of formulae that admit no hesitation or complexity. One must not be long-winded when one issues a command requiring immediate response. The drill sergeant does not indulge in discussion.

The house-owner is asked, ahead of time, to set up a table close to the front door, and to cover it with a white cloth.

For the exorcist, the first task is to gather together all the implements and supplies that are necessary, and place them within your bag. Exorcists must take a number of things with them – salt, water, bread, wine, flowers, candles, coins, oil, stick incense, an incense-burner and a chalice. (Instructions for preparing these things are given in the introduction, under the heading 'Equipment for the Hunt and for the Rite'.)

Personal preparations for any ritual can be as simple as washing your hands, brushing your teeth or lighting a candle, but if it is not a routine one, it is better to do more.

First, if you are a woman, freshen your make-up, brush your hair, put on perfume and clean clothes and wear one of your better pairs of shoes. This is almost a matter of simple good manners. Men should dress more neatly than usual and take a little care over the rest of their appearance.

However, if the ritual is as important as an exorcism, more

preparation is required. It is necessary to satisfy the everyday world and to be prepared to step into a different space one that is, as we say in some of our rituals, 'a place that is not a place, and a time that is not a time'.

Take a bath before the ceremony, to break the electromagnetic energy picked up in the routine of the day, especially if you work with computers or machines. Add to the bathwater one cup of salt, soda or vinegar. You may use whichever appeals to you. If in doubt, taste them all, and one taste will feel appropriate. As you bathe, let everyday problems float away; concentrate on being clear; dress in fresh clothes that are special to you and that are loose and comfortable. (Jean prefers long skirts.) If you have long hair, leave it down, flowing loosely; there should be no combs or pins or knots in it. Anoint all the body openings with protection oil, and drink several glasses of water with lemon in it; this is to increase the alkali content of your body, which also increases your psychic ability.

Chant the words, 'Ishtar, Demeter, Rjamet, Isis, Astarte, Diana, Hecate, Ananna, By the virtue of these sacred names do I clothe myself, Great Mother, in my ritual robes and oil, that in them I shall perform all the desires and services to others that you require of me. In your name, and with your gracious aid, this is my wish, and as I wish, so must it be.'

This is the formula to use in matters of love, hearth and home. For other occasions, outdoors or dealing with curses, you should probably invoke the male God's names. This, at least, is how witches would operate. If you are unsympathetic to the Old Religion, other names can, of course, be used. One could even avoid any reference to deity of any kind and begin the incantation with the sound 'Om' or some other vibrant sound that you sense appropriate.

The two assistants arrive at the house carrying bundles of stick incense. Jean stands behind her assistants, holding a candle which has been lit with a wooden or paper match, not with a cigarette-lighter. The visitors knock on the door, and the house-owner invites the group inside.

Jean and her guest remain on the threshold at the open front door as the two assistants, turning outward to face the walls of the house, begin their task. They trace a circle around the inside of the house with their burning sticks of incense, letting the smoke of the incense touch every bit of the outside wall, one going in one direction and one in the other, so that eventually they meet and their paths cross, thus sealing the whole of that floor of the house. They then go upstairs, where they follow the same procedure, ensuring that each of them has covered the whole of the house's perimeter. The same circling is carried out also in the basement. Particular care is taken to ensure that all windows and openings upon the outside world are covered, not forgetting whatever trapdoor there may be into the roof space. When they have completed these circuits, they return to the open front door, where Jean and her guest are standing on the threshold. Jean steps forward followed by her guest, the door is closed and the two assistants complete their task by passing the incense smoke over the door, crossing each other's path, thus completing the sealing of the house and trapping whatever presence or entity has been disturbing it in the circle which they have made.

Now that the circle has been completed and the house sealed, and the table has been furnished with what is necessary, Jean performs a preparatory protective ritual with the oil, anointing the third eye of everyone present, with the words: 'I consecrate this oil of the purest plants so that you may aid me in my task; as I wish so it must be.'

Another version of this consecration is: 'To Diana, protectress of the innocent, with this oil may I purify and renew my purpose that all deeds performed by me shall be for the good of us all. As I wish, so must it be.'

A third and very old one runs:

> Now this oily essence fair
> adds its power to the air,
> attracting spirits of the light,
> protecting us both day and night.
> This charge is true and proper be
> and as I wish, so must it be.

With the middle finger of your right hand anoint your third eye, so that you shall be doubly protected.

The candles are now lit, and the incense is ignited. The candles must be lit with a wooden or paper match, never with a cigarette-lighter. The following words should be said:

> Creature of fire, this charge I give.
> No phantom in your presence live.
> Hear my will addressed to thee,
> And as I wish, so must it be.

As the candles (appropriate to the particular person or entity being addressed) are being lit, Jean says: 'In the name of light may this person be released from all controlling energies and received into the great wholeness of perfect harmony and peace.'

The water is then exorcized by Jean with the words: 'I exorcize you, creature of water, that you shall cast out all the impurities and uncleanliness of the spirits of this world and of all phantoms. This I ask in the name of Goodness and Mercy.'

For exorcism Jean prefers to use the phrase 'Goodness and Mercy' rather than some Goddess name, because the people present may feel uneasy at other names, having been brought up in a different religious tradition. Also, while everyone can empathize with an appeal to 'Goodness and Mercy', many people would find themselves automatically resisting such names as Isis, Diana and Gaea. It is important that those present should not only understand what is happening but feel able to share in the proceedings. Mumbo-jumbo would be counter-productive. On the other hand, if the householders are practitioners of a particular religion and firm believers in it, Jean uses words appropriate to that religion.

The salt does not need to be exorcized, for salt is the spiritual equivalent of all antiseptics and cleansers. It is therefore never exorcized, but it is blessed with the words: 'Blessing be upon this spirit of salt Let all malignancy and hindrance be cast forth, and let all goodness enter herein. Let us ever be reminded that as water and salt purify the body, so turbulence must purify the soul. Therefore I bless you, that you may aid me in the name of Goodness and Mercy.' In this blessing the word 'turbulence' is used to indicate energetic psychic activity.

Salt is then dipped or poured into the water and mixed with the middle finger of the right hand and stirred deosil (clockwise). 'It is,' Jean says, 'a bit like baking a cake. There is a moment when you know the consistency is right.'

> Water and salt, where you are cast,
> no spell or unknown purpose last
> not in complete accord with
> [*the names of the house-owners*].
> As they wish, so must it be.

The word 'spell' is used here because it is a general term encompassing cursing, haunting and all other forms of intended psychic disturbance.

> Spirits of this water holy
> light upon these objects only;
> sanctify them as you should
> and consecrate them for our good.

> In the name of the unnamed God, and Goddess who dwell within us all, I conjure thee, all helpful and friendly spirits: draw nigh and attend us!
> We crave and desire your loving protection and influence this night to assist us in our desire to free and cleanse this house from all unhappy memories and distressing emotions. Draw nigh and place your benevolent protection about us!
> Enfold us in a protective cone of power!
> Let no harm come to the bodies, the minds, the spirits, the souls, of me and my companions who attend me! We ask this in the name of Goodness and Mercy.

The group is then asked: 'Do you feel safe and protected?' If anyone says 'No', the conjuration is repeated until they all feel secure. Then Jean asks them, 'Shall I continue?', and if they all say 'Yes', Jean goes on with the next stage of the exorcism, saying:

> Spirits of the dead that dwell in this house, attend me!
> Elemental spirits of the woods that draw nigh to this house, attend me!
> Spirits of the water beneath and above and around this house, dryads and undines, attend me!
> Spirits of fire and salamanders that enter this house, attend me!
> Living spirits of the animals from the woods and the birds of the air, attend me!
> Energy produced by anger and envy, appear before me!
> Energy produced by fear, resentment, frustration, desolation, illness and imprisonment, appear before me!
> All thought-forms produced by lustful and unclean thoughts directed against the people who dwell in this house, appear before me!
> Submit unto my will and stand before me!
> As I command, so must it be!

The presence may show itself visibly, as a spectre or a shadow, or it may cause a candle flame to flare or flicker. In some instances there is no physical manifestation at all but simply a sense of something or someone being present.

This conjuration is repeated until everyone in the group feels the presence. Then Jean says:

> In the name of the unnamed God and Goddess that dwell within us all, I adjure you that you shall appear before me, visibly and invisibly. You are no longer confined to this earthly plane. Let loose all tentacles of fear and despair, and draw yourself upwards towards the light, let no remnant remain behind you. All emotions and material desires that blind you to this place are severed.
> I command you to leave this place and to rise upwards, always upwards, into the light.
> Go ever upwards to the light, where you will find loving comfort and guidance. This is my command and as I wish, so must it be!

This is also repeated as many times as necessary until everyone feels that the presence is gone. The house is then blessed with the words:

> Spirit of Bread, fill these empty rooms with your essence that all hungers are satisfied and no one is ever turned away hungry from this door.
> Spirit of the flowers, fill these empty rooms with your fragrance and beauty that all who dwell here will be inspired.
> Spirit of the wine, fill these empty rooms with your essence of hospitality and joyous celebration.

When this has been said, the two assistants take the salt and water and anoint all the windows, all the doors, the light switches, heating vents and anything that provides an opening of any kind to the outside world. Then Jean asks everyone attending the ceremony to take some item from the table and carry it to where he or she considers the heart of the house to be. There they put whatever they are carrying in a place they feel appropriate and say some form of blessing. Different people pick different rooms: one may decide on the kitchen, one on the living-room, one on a bedroom or even the top of the stairs.

These blessings are important, for at this point the house is a vacuum. It has been completely emptied and must be filled again immediately, leaving no room for anything unhappy to seep back in.

The group then meets together and discusses how everyone is feeling. Is there any place that anyone feels is still a little uncomfortable? If so, first-aid in the form of a strong blessing is given to that particular place. After which this the concluding words are:

> All elemental spirits gathered here, I thank you for your help and participation. Now go in peace back to your native habitat and harm no one on your way. Thank you also to the spirit beings who help me always.
> In the name of the unnamed God and Goddess that dwells within us all, we thank you for your protection and loving kindness. Continue your benevolent protection of this house and all who dwell within. I release you now with our grateful thanks to return to your own plane of existence until I shall have need of you again. This is my command, and as I command, so must it be!

This having been done, the company then have a feast of some kind.

It is extremely important, during this surge of celebratory feelings, that the householders be warned that there may be residual disturbances during the coming twenty-four hours. The lights may go on and off; there may be sudden noises, and doors that open and close by themselves. This is because the energy field in the house has been disturbed and is readjusting itself. There is nothing to be afraid of. It does not mean that the exorcism has failed, but rather the reverse.

Jean also tells the householders to let the whole episode and the previous disturbances out of their minds. They must not think about these matters or dwell on them or talk about them. Every time one remembers and dwells upon a haunting, it is possible that the disturbing presence may be drawn back to the house.